SCIENCE FICTION FILMS

Endpapers *The spaceship lands in **Close Encounters of the Third Kind** (1977).*

This page *Keir Dallea on the "Cosmic Ride" in **2001 – A Space Odyssey** (1968).*

Pages 2–3 *David Warner as Sark in **Tron** (1982).*

Pages 4–5 *Space battles in **The Empire Strikes Back** (1980).*

This book was devised and produced by Multimedia Publications (UK) Ltd

Editor: Richard Rosenfeld
Assistant editor: Sydney Francis
Production: Karen Bromley
Design: Michael Hodson Designs
Picture Research: David Sutherland

Copyright © Multimedia Publications (UK) Ltd 1985

First published in the United States of America 1985 by Gallery Books, an imprint of W. H. Smith Publishers Inc., 112 Madison Avenue, New York, NY 10016

ISBN 0 8317 7713 3

Typeset by Letterspace Ltd
Origination by The Clifton Studio Ltd, London
Printed in Italy by Sagdos

SCIENCE FICTION
FILMS

ROBIN CROSS

GALLERY BOOKS
An Imprint of W. H. Smith Publishers Inc.
112 Madison Avenue
New York City 10016

CONTENTS

COPYRIGHTED
BY GEO. MÉLIÈS 1906
PARIS NEW-YORK
Trade-Mark ★ Star

6

Introduction

Science fiction films are almost as old as the cinema itself. Nevertheless, for most of their early history scant attention was paid to them, either by movie critics or by the fans of science fiction literature. Even among movie buffs they were all too often relegated to a kind of B-movie ghetto in which Fritz Lang's magnificent **Metropolis** (1926) rubbed shoulders with **Monster From the Ocean Floor** (1954) or **Creature With the Atom Brain** (1955). Despite impressive productions like **The War of the Worlds** (1953) and **This Island Earth** (1955), science fiction was associated with minimal budgets, tottering sets, laughable special effects and fading stars reduced to virtual incoherence by the absurdities of the plot.

But the science fiction film has struck back. In the 1960s the genre became "respectable" and was taken up by Jean-Luc Godard in **Alphaville** (1965) and François Truffaut in **Fahrenheit 451** (1966). The process was completed at the end of the decade by three big-budget films: Roger Vadim's **Barbarella** (1967), Stanley Kubrick's **2001: A Space Odyssey** (1968) and Franklin Schaffner's **Planet of the Apes** (1968). The last, with its huge box-office success and four sequels,

pointed the way to the boom of the late 1970s, when a series of megahits established science fiction as Hollywood's most popular genre.

The impetus was maintained into the 1980s and by mid-decade showed no sign of slacking. In 1984 *Variety* published a list of the 20 all-time box-office hits. Occupying the first four positions were science fiction films: **E.T. The Extra-Terrestrial** (1982), **Star Wars** (1977), **Return of the Jedi** (1983) and **The Empire Strikes Back** (1980). Science fiction films have taken a firm grip on the popular imagination: so much so that the No. 2 film in *Variety*'s list has provided President Reagan with a convenient shorthand description of the latest twist in the strategic arms spiral, the development of satellite battle stations in space – a case of life imitating art with a vengeance.

Left *A shoal of mermaids in Georges Méliès' engaging fantasy* **20,000 Leagues Under the Sea,** *very loosely based on Jules Verne's novel of the same name.* **Below** *Jeff Morrow, Rex Reason, Faith Domergue and a dying inhabitant of the planet Metaluna in* **This Island Earth** *(1955).*

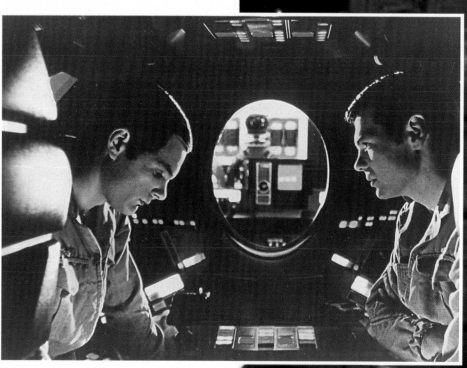

Above *Keir Dullea and Gary Lockwood in Stanley Kubrick's **2001: A Space Odyssey** (1968), the most influential science fiction film of the 1960s. Lockwood also turned up in the sequel **2010** (1985).* **Below Planet of the Apes** *(1968), which examined the forces controlling Man's evolution.*
Right *The good ship Enterprise on a rendezvous with destiny in **Star Trek – The Motion Picture** (1979), directed by Robert Wise.* **Top right** *Donald Sutherland fatally slumbers next to his alien replacement in the 1978 remake of Don Siegel's classic **Invasion of the Body Snatchers** (1956). One of the film's most deft touches was the casting of Star Trek veteran Leonard Nimoy as a fashionable psychiatrist taken over by an alien intelligence.*

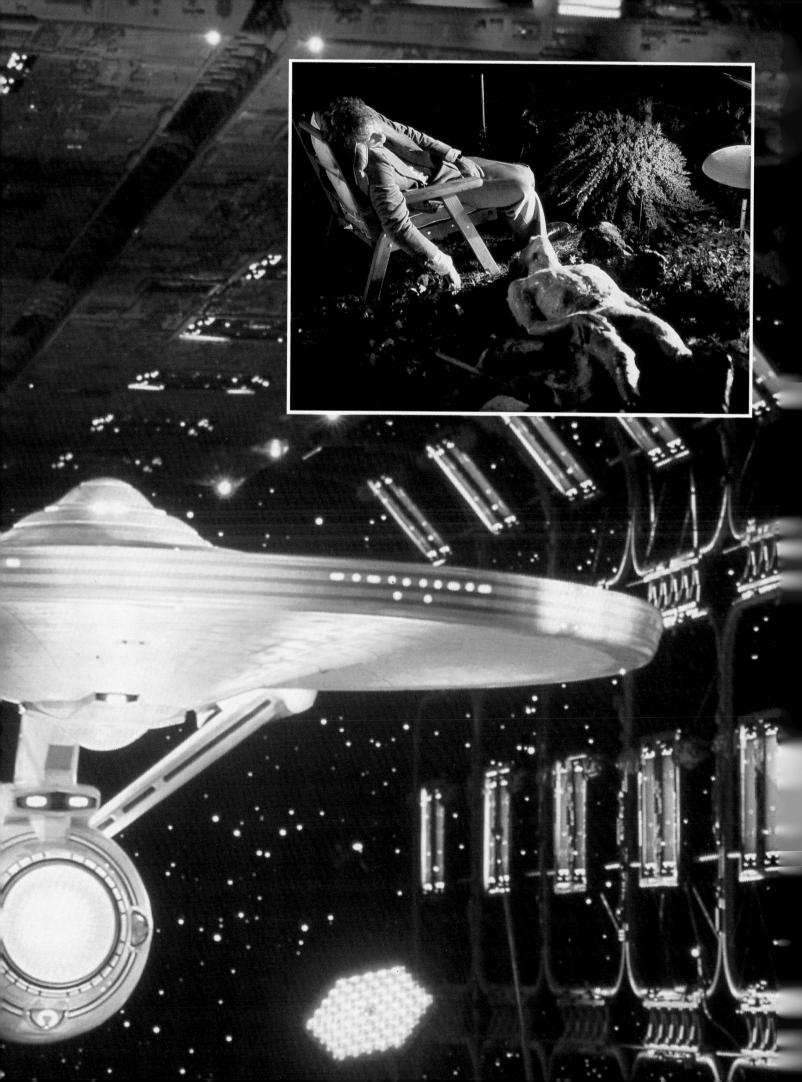

CHAPTER ONE

The Great Pioneers

To trace **Star Wars** back to its humble origins, we must travel back in time some 90 years to turn-of-the-century Paris. The first recorded example of a science fiction film is **The Mechanical Butcher** (1895), a 60-second humorous short made in France by the Lumière brothers. The machine of the title is a wonder of modern science, a large box into which a live pig is manhandled at one end. It emerges at the other conveniently converted into a selection of bacon, sausages, hams and spare ribs.

Trick photography
In the early days, filmmakers devoted much time and ingenuity to the development of the trick photography with which they made the impossible happen before their audience's eyes. The French showman Georges Méliès was among the most skillful, experimenting with many of the basic techniques – stop-motion photography, the matte process, multiple exposures – which still lie at the heart of the special effects in today's fantasy movies.

Stop-motion and double exposure were used by Méliès in his **Les Rayons Roentgen** (or **A Novice at X-Rays**, 1897), a satire on W.A. Roentgen's discovery of invisible penetrative rays. A doctor, played by Méliès himself, X-rays a patient. The patient's skeleton appears and then jumps out of his body while his flesh slumps to the floor.

Early films with strong science fiction elements – like the British **The Elixir of Life** (1901), which exploited the theme of rejuvenation – were little more than one-minute humorous items. In Robert Paul's **An Over-Incubated Baby** (1901), an incubator normally used for hatching chicks is adapted by a professor for human use. It bears the encouraging legend: "Two Years' Growth in Two Minutes". A sickly mite is placed in the incubator, but the professor's assistant upsets the controls and the baby emerges as a senile man.

Early epics
The inventive Méliès also produced the world's first science fiction epic. Lasting just over 20 minutes, **La Voyage dans la Lune** (**Voyage to the Moon**, 1902) absorbed all of his skills as a master of illusion. He

Below *Georges Méliès'* **La Voyage dans la Lune** (**Voyage to the Moon**, *1902*), *the first science fiction epic.* **Right** *Slightly less than epic. Statuesque alien Patricia Laffan emerges from her spacecraft to scour the Scottish countryside for male earthlings to service her Martian matriarchy in the awful* **Devil Girl from Mars** *(1954).* **Inset** *Fritz Lang's* **Dr. Mabuse der Spieler** (**Dr. Mabuse the Gambler**, *1922*), *whose master villain used hypnotic and telepathic powers to further his evil ends.*

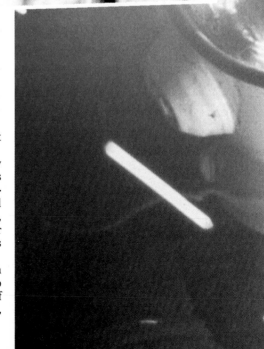

Above *E.E. Clive's walrus-mustached Police Constable Jaffers confronts Claude Rains in* **The Invisible Man** *(1933).* **Right** *As Earth is threatened by the roving star Bellus a rocketship of survivors takes off in George Pal's* **When Worlds Collide** *(1951).* **Far right** **Outland** *(1981), a space remake of* **High Noon** *(1952)—see overleaf.*

also took the leading role of Professor Barbenfouillis, whose plan for the exploration of the Moon is accepted by the Scientific Congress of the Astronomic Club.

Méliès happily plundered both Jules Verne's *From the Earth to the Moon* and H. G. Wells' *First Men in the Moon* for the film's cheerful storyline. He used Verne's huge cannon to hurl the explorers' space shell to the Moon where they encounter Wells' underground race of aliens, the Selenites, who take them prisoner. They escape, having made the fortunate discovery that their captors explode in a puff of smoke as soon as they are struck. The return journey to Earth ends with a splashdown in the sea and a whistle-stop tour of the wonders of the deep. The explorers are rescued by a passing ship and return in triumph to Paris.

The ebullient Méliès also cast himself in the lead, as Engineer Maboulouff, in his **Voyage à Travers l'Impossible** (**An Impossible Voyage**, 1904). This time the Sun was the destination and the spacecraft a strange hybrid conveyance which served, at different times, as railway train, airship and submarine. Lifting off from the Jungfrau by means of airships attached to the railway carriages, the explorers head straight for the smiling face of the Sun.

Laying down the rules

By 1910 many of the enduring themes of science fiction cinema were steadily evolving. Méliès' **La Voyage dans la Lune** had established space travel and contact with hostile aliens, and **The Airship Destroyer** had mapped out the future-war scenario. The future-war theme was taken up in British films, such as **An Englishman's Home** (1914) and **If England Were Invaded** (1914), at a time when the possibilities flickering on the screen were fast becoming reality in the world outside.

The theme of invisibility, inspired by Wells' *The Invisible Man* (1898), was explored in the American short **The Invisible Fluid** (1908) and the delightful French comedy **An Invisible Thief** (1909), whose masterly special effects were later used by John P. Fulton in Hollywood's **The Invisible Man** (1933).

The Monkey Man (1908), made in France, was one of the first films to illustrate brain transplants. The transfer of brains from ape to man, and vice versa,

12

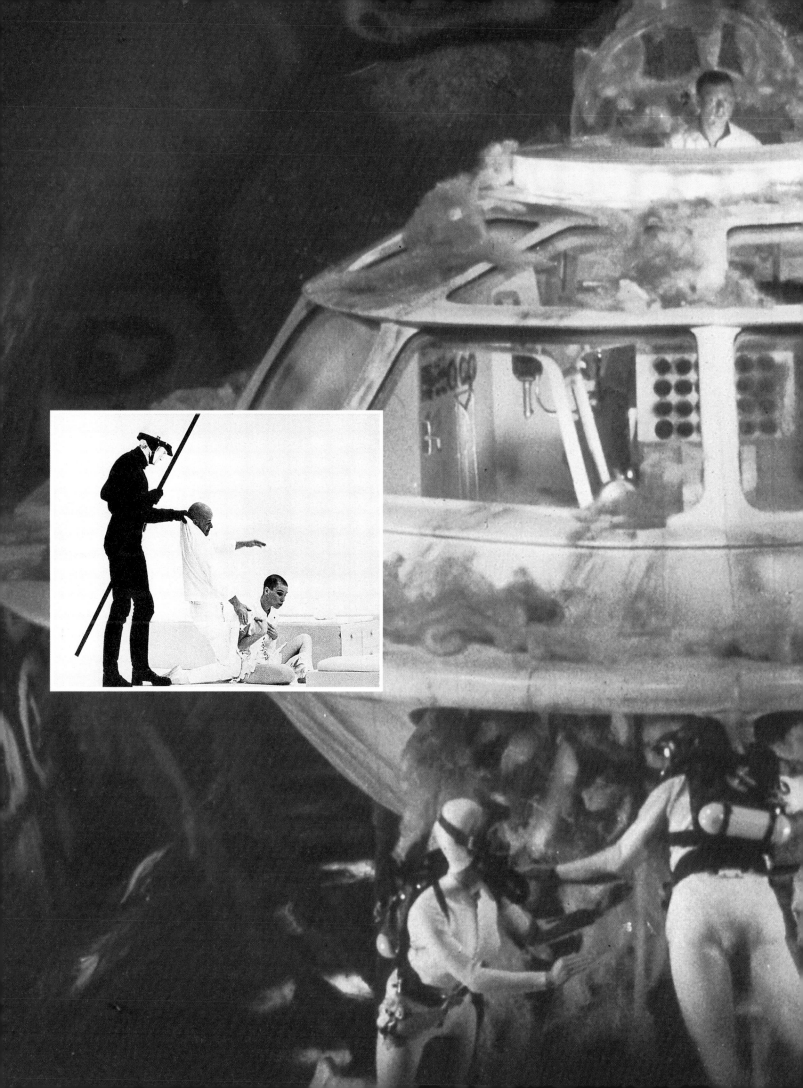

was to become a particular favorite of 1940s B-features in such low-budget outings as **The Monster and the Girl** (1941), **Dr. Renault's Secret** (1942) and **Jungle Captive** (1944). This theme was also bound up with that of loss of individuality, a rich seam running through science fiction films from the hypnotism of Lang's **Dr. Mabuse, der Spieler** (**Dr. Mabuse, the Gambler**, 1922) to the possession of human beings by alien lookalikes grown in pods in Don Siegel's **Invasion of the Body Snatchers** (1956).

The application of scientific method to the increasing of brain power was the subject of Sigmund Lubin's **Professor Weise's Brain Serum Injector** (1909). The notion finds a distant echo in **Charly** (1968), in which a subnormal man is briefly and poignantly turned into a genius.

Cosmic destruction

The American film **The Comet** (1910), in which Halley's Comet plunges out of its orbit and hurtles past the Earth, leaving a trail of devastation in its wake, anticipated George Pal's **When Worlds Collide** (1951) and the 1970s disaster movie **Meteor** (1979). Lubin's comedy **The Rubber Man** (1909) devised a robot-like creature which owed more to pure science fiction than to the Coppélia legend of dancing automata. It was the first of countless movie robots to go berserk, tossing its inventor and his family out of the window and then stuffing an old woman up a chimney. After it is dunked in a water trough, the humanoid's electrical circuits are fused, rendering him harmless.

This wide range of subjects – invisibility, brain transplants, space travel, artificial intelligence and cosmic disasters – opens up the question of the limits to science fiction film. It is an infinitely flexible form. Like the hungry alien protoplasm which casually eats the inhabitants of a small American town in **The Blob** (1958), science fiction film is capable of absorbing and adapting other movie genres. The extraordinary **Phantom Empire** (1935) is derived from the singing cowboy B-features of the 1930s, while **Outland** (1981) is a straightforward remake of **High Noon** (1952), complete with digital clocks counting down the moments before the arrival on Sean Connery's space station of the hired killers.

Contemplating the unthinkable

By and large the Western takes place in the American West, from about 1830 to 1914. But science fiction can be located in the distant past (**The Spaceman and King Arthur**, 1979) or in the distant future (**THX 1138**, 1970); in deepest space (**Silent Running**, 1971) or inside the human body (**Fantastic Voyage**, 1966) or the innards of a super-computer (**Tron**, 1982); on a vast aircraft platform moored in the mid-Atlantic (**F P 1 Doesn't Answer**, 1932) or in an arctic research station (**The Thing**, 1951).

The function of science fiction is to imagine the impossible, or to contemplate the unthinkable. The onward rush of technology has adjusted the terms of reference – the devastation caused by an airship raid pales beside the "Arctic Winter" that will follow a nuclear exchange – but the themes remain unchanged.

Far left *THX 1138 (1970), George Lucas' directorial debut, set in a sterile underground dystopia patrolled by mechanical policemen.* **Left** *Inner space – the minisub Proteus voyages through a scientist's body in* **Fantastic Voyage** *(1966).* **Below** *Outer space – the last ecologist Bruce Dern and his robot helpers create a stellar Garden of Eden after Earth is destroyed by nuclear war in* **Silent Running** *(1971).*

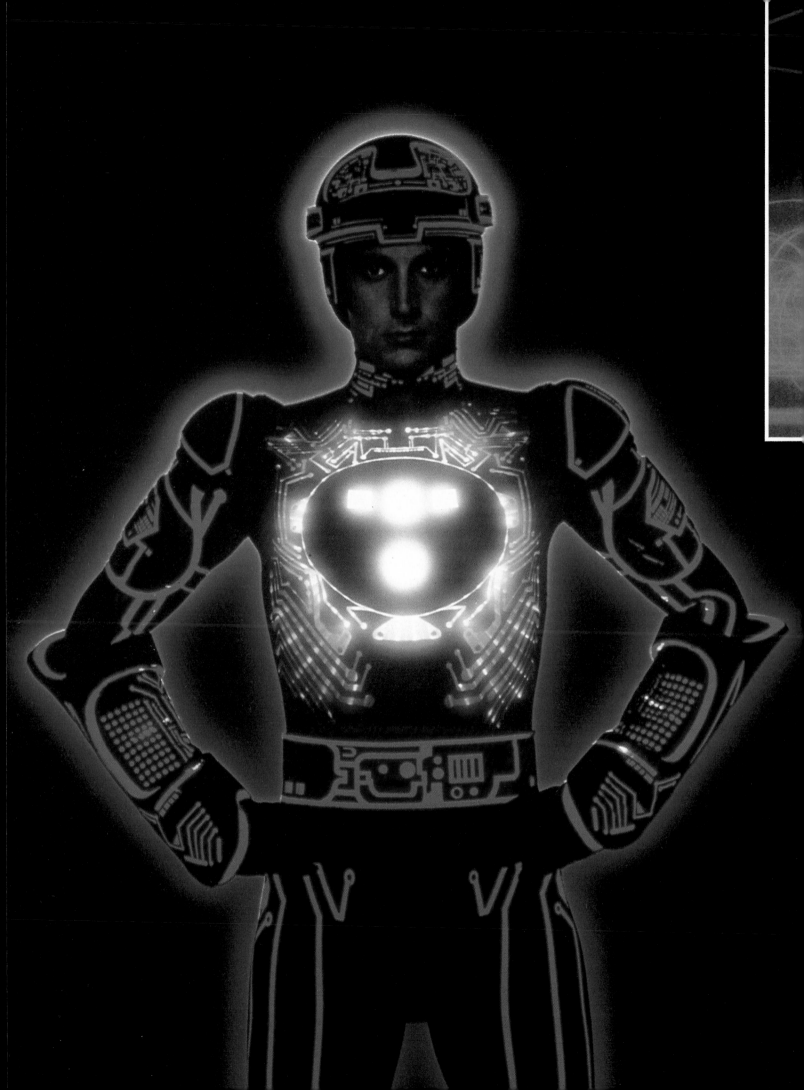

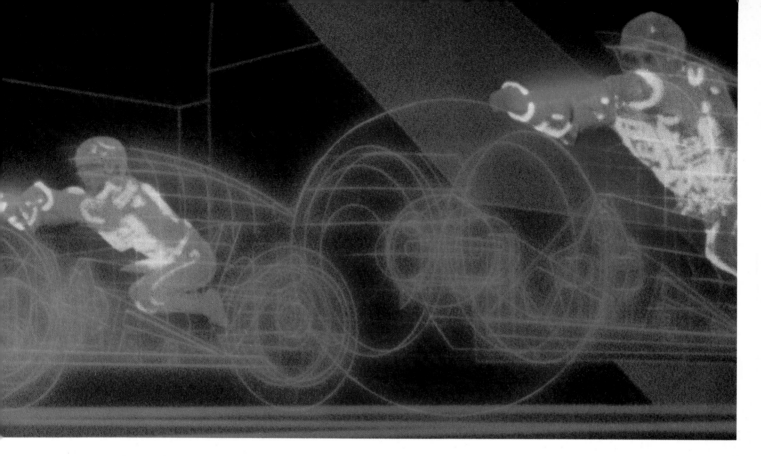

In spite of their quaintness, many of the early science fiction films were often inspired by technical advances that at the time seemed as startling as the breakthroughs of the present day. The arguments over Darwinian theory, humorously portrayed in **The Monkey Man**, have now moved on to the cloning experiments depicted in **The Boys From Brazil** (1978).

Hollywood to Homunculus
During the First World War the Hollywood studio system was beginning to take shape. In 1915 Carl Laemmle opened Universal City, then the biggest studio in the world. Under the influence of the film capital's production line, science fiction themes were combined with laughs and fast-paced action to provide straightforward popular entertainment. Typical of the science-fiction-tinged movies of the period was **The Exploits of Elaine** (1914), the first in a snappy run of serials starring Pearl White and Arnold Daly as a gadget-obsessed scientific detective.

From a technical point of view, the outstanding American science fiction film at this time was Universal's **Twenty Thousand Leagues Under the Sea** (1916), which includes some stunning underwater photography filmed in a huge tank in a studio in Nassau and unmatched until the same team of technicians worked on

MGM's **The Mysterious Island** (1929), the first of five adaptations of Verne's sequel to his *20,000 Leagues Under the Sea.*

Hollywood's breezy attiude towards science fiction contrasts sharply with the prevailing mood in Germany, which was more concerned with the bizarre and the grotesque than with uncritical celebrations of the wonders of technology. Paul Wegener's **Der Golem** (1914) reached back

into the past and was the first of a number of films based on the legend of the lumbering clay statue brought to life in sixteenth-century Prague by the magician Rabbi Loew. Dissatisfied with the updated setting of the film, Wegener remade **Der Golem** in 1920. A classic of silent cinema, **Der Golem**'s monster greatly influenced James Whale's **Frankenstein** (1931).

Another important film in the German

Left and above *Tron (1982), directed by Steven Lisberg, was a video version of* **Fantastic Voyage** *in which Jeff Bridges ventured inside a computer's circuits.* **Right** *René Clair's charming* **Paris Qui Dort (The Crazy Ray**, *1923), in which a scientist's invisible ray freezes Paris into immobility.*

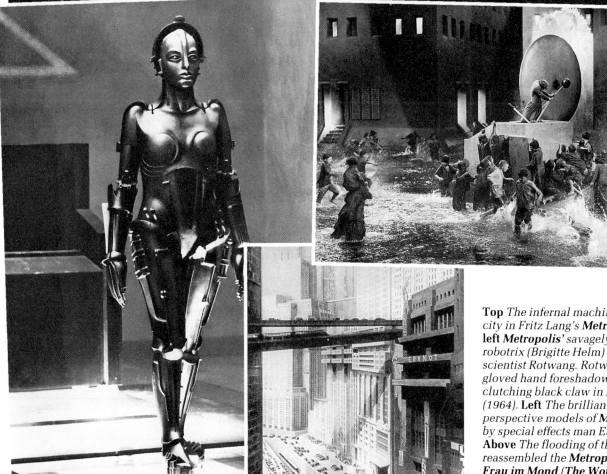

Top *The infernal machinery of the lower city in Fritz Lang's* **Metropolis** *(1926).* **Far left** *Metropolis'* *savagely beautiful robotrix (Brigitte Helm) created by the scientist Rotwang. Rotwang's deformed gloved hand foreshadows Peter Sellers' clutching black claw in* **Dr. Strangelove** *(1964).* **Left** *The brilliant forced perspective models of* **Metropolis** *created by special effects man Eugen Schuefftan.* **Above** *The flooding of the lower city. Lang reassembled the* **Metropolis** *team for* **Die Frau im Mond (The Woman in the Moon,** *1929), in which an expedition travels to the Moon to prospect for gold.*

artificial creature cycle is Otto Rippert's **Homunculus** (1916), a serial in six one-hour chapters. In his laboratory a scientist (Friedrich Kuehne) creates a "perfect" creature (Olaf Foenss) of pure reason and will – Homunculus. When Homunculus discovers that he has no soul, he revenges himself on mankind, in the process becoming an all-powerful tyrant. In the end Homunculus is destroyed by a bolt of lightning.

The road to Metropolis

One of Rippert's assistants on **Homunculus** was Fritz Lang. Trained as an architect, he had been invalided out of the First World War and had turned his hand to screen-writing. Soon he began to direct his own films, and in **Die Spinnen (The Spiders**, 1919) Lang created a two-part fantasy adventure story that remained unsurpassed until Steven Spielberg's **Raiders of the Lost Ark** (1981).

In 1924 Lang visited America to study Hollywood production methods, and it was the sight of the Manhattan skyline at night that gave him the idea for **Metropolis** (1926). This film became one of the landmarks in cinema, and was a science fiction movie whose scope and ingenuity remained unrivaled until Kubrick's **2001: A Space Odyssey** (1968).

A vision of the future

Metropolis was conceived on a scale to rival the mega-productions of the 1980s. At a time when most films were made in a few weeks at most, the shooting of **Metropolis** stretched over 16 months with a cast of 37,000.

The scale of the production was matched by Lang's vision of the future. **Metropolis** is set at the end of the century in a colossal city ruled by a remote industrialist, John Fredersen (Alfred Abel). Fredersen is a benevolent version of Lang's criminal genius Dr. Mabuse, his office looking down over the dizzying skyscraper canyons of his kingdom. The Utopian luxury enjoyed by the city's élite is made possible by the teeming workforce in the catacombs below. They lead lives of endless drudgery in a labyrinth of monstrous machines, a picture of technology gone berserk and horribly inhuman.

Fredersen's son visits the lower city where he finds the saintly Maria (Brigitte Helm) who preaches peaceful revolution, comparing Metropolis to the Tower of Babel. The all-seeing Fredersen plans to nip the revolt in the bud and instructs his chief scientist Rotwang (Rudolf Klein-Rogge) to build a robot replica of Maria: "We have made machines out of men – now we will make men out of machines." The result is a work of savage beauty, brought to life by a dramatic electrical charge and then covered with synthetic flesh.

The robot Maria incites the workers to revolt. They embark on an orgy of destruction, smashing the mechanical heart of the city and flooding its lower levels, with great loss of life. Finally they turn on the

Above left *The director Vsevolod Pudovkin as the villain in **Luch Smerti** (**The Death Ray**, 1925), an energetic Soviet foray into science fiction. Another key Soviet sf adventure of the period was **Aelita** (1924), in which some astronauts foment a revolution on Mars.* **Above** *Paul Wegener as **The Golem** (1920), the lumbering clay giant brought to life by the Rabbi Loew in 16th-century Prague. A film of haunting beauty, it straddled the science fiction and horror genres. The influence of the Golem's make-up can clearly be seen in the Monster played by Boris Karloff in **Frankenstein** (1931).*

robot Maria and burn her at the stake, only to gaze horrified as the flesh peels away to reveal the pitiless metal mast underneath. The real Maria escapes with Fredersen's son, and the film concludes with a tentative reconciliation between the workers and the city's rulers. Love, the greatest mediator of them all, has effected a rather unconvincing alliance between capital and labor.

The greatness of **Metropolis** lies in Lang's ability to rise above the puerile storyline and present the audience with a series of stunning cinematic effects – from the geometrically choreographed armies of shuffling, bowed workers to Rotwang's torchlit pursuit of Maria through the city's foundations. In keeping with Lang's early training, the film boasts many superb architectural settings.

CHAPTER TWO

Vision Of Things To Come

In the years leading up to the Second World War European science fiction films followed the path of prophetic speculation laid out by **Metropolis**. In France Abel Gance directed **La Fin du Monde** (**The End of the World**, 1930), in which a comet hurtles towards Earth amid a wave of orgiastic looting and a succession of natural disasters. **FP1 Antwortet Nicht** (**FP1 Doesn't Answer**, 1932) was one of a number of German films to hymn a heroic engineering venture.

The FP1 of the title is a vast aircraft platform moored in the mid-Atlantic on which airplanes refuel during their Europe–American flights. Basically a simple-minded flying ace adventure, the film is dominated by the massive set of the aircraft platform. A small touch on a human scale was provided by Peter Lorre's tragi-comic performance as a reporter.

The British **Non Stop New York** (1937), directed by Robert Stevenson, looked forward to jet travel across the Atlantic by 1940. **Q-Planes** (1939), directed by Tim Whelan, was a jaunty thriller in which test pilot Laurence Olivier and detective Ralph Richardson foil a spy ring's plot to destroy Britain's new bomber fleet with a death ray. Despite its absurd storyline, **Q-Planes** accurately predicted the role of the bomber in the Second World War.

Der Tunnel (**The Tunnel**, 1935), directed by Kurt (later Curtis) Bernhardt, followed the driving of a tunnel under the Atlantic to connect Europe and the United States. A crooked speculator tries to blow up the tunnel, causing a spectacular flood

and the deaths of hundreds of workers, but the project is finally finished. Two years later the veteran British director Maurice Elvey produced **Transatlantic Tunnel** (1937), a carbon copy of **Der Tunnel**, starring stern-jawed American leading man Richard Dix. While the German film struck an ultra-patriotic and militaristic note, Elvey chose to dwell on the problems encountered by engineer Dix and his family. Nevertheless, the special effects – nearly all of which were achieved with models – are remarkably effective, particularly a gigantic "radium drill" churning through the ocean bed.

Future imperfect

The most important European science fiction film of the decade – and one of the most important of any decade – was William Cameron Menzies' **Things to Come** (1936). This ambitious project was adapted for the cinema by H. G. Wells from his own *The Shape of Things to Come*, and its dated view of the future and hazy philosophizing owe much to Wells' dominating influence over the film and

Below FP1 Antwortet Nicht (FP1 Doesn't Answer, 1932). Right Raymond Massey contemplates the Universe in William Cameron Menzies' Things to Come (1936). Inset The bland art deco lines of Things to Come's technological Utopia of 2036. Menzies' genius as a production designer is evident throughout the film.

his inexperience as a screenwriter. This presented Menzies – who was better known as a production designer – with almost insuperable problems on his first directorial assignment. The film is saved by Menzies' sheer brilliance as a designer and a sterling central performance by Raymond Massey.

Things to Come opens in 1940 with a massed bombing raid on "Everytown", which is clearly meant to be London. What was considered to be almost science fiction at the time was to become reality in the space of four years. The scene moves on to the late 1960s to reveal a rubble-strewn and crater-pitted Everytown ruled over by the "Boss", a fur-clad fascist warlord played with great relish by Ralph Richardson. His brutal reign is brought to an end by John Cabal (Massey), a representative of a society of scientists, the Airmen, who are rebuilding the world. "Who are you?" demands the Boss. "Law and Sanity," Cabal replies. "I *am* the Law," blusters the Boss. "I said *'Law and Sanity'*," is the stern reply.

Technological Utopia
The Boss is not long for this world, as Cabal's "peace gas" transforms Everytown's savage population into model citizens while at the same time killing their brutal ruler. In its final segment, **Things to Come** moves on to 2036, presenting us with a highly developed technological Utopia. Its bland, clean, art deco

lines hint at an immensely dull society. Moreover, the benevolent authoritarianism of its scientific elite sails perilously close to fascism. A sculptor, played by Cedric Hardwicke, advocates a return to the past, when "life was short, hot and merry". But Oswald Cabal (John Cabal's grandson, also played by Massey) places his faith in sending humanity into space, using a giant electrical cannon. (This impressive machine looks back to Méliès' **La Voyage dans la Lune** and, ironically, forward to the electromagnetic space catapult developed during the 1980s by the Massachusetts Institute of Techology.)

A mob led by Hardwicke attempts to sabotage the cannon, but at the last moment Cabal succeeds in firing it and its human cargo into space.

Seeing the Invisible Man
In the United States the course of science fiction cinema in the 1930s was determined by two big box-office failures: Fox's futuristic musical **Just Imagine** (1930), and the same studio's **It's Great to be Alive** (1933). A loose reworking of the silent **The Last Man on Earth** (1924), **It's Great to be Alive** qualifies as one of the most bizarre sf movies ever made.

An aviator crash-lands on a deserted Pacific island, and as a result escapes a strange disease, "masculitis", which kills off the entire male population of the world. Within four years, however, it is business as usual, but run entirely by women. Our hero is kidnapped by a female version of Al Capone who plans to auction him off to the dowagers of New York. But the police have other plans for him, as a stud with a worldwide role. In a conventional ending he is reunited with his sweetheart.

These two offbeat failures and the poor reception of RKO's **The Deluge** (1933) – in which New York is destroyed by a combination of earthquake and tidal wave – discouraged the big Hollywood studios from producing expensive science fiction movies. Universal's **The Invisible Man** (1933), based on Wells' novel, was not to have a sequel until 1940. A stylish black comedy, wittily scripted by R.C. Sherriff and directed by James Whale, **The Invisible Man** starred Claude Rains as the scientist who is deranged by the side-effects of his invisibility serum.

To John P. Fulton's polished special effects – particularly memorable in the scene in which the Invisible Man peels the

Below *Una O'Connor about to get a nasty surprise in James Whale's* **The Invisible Man** *(1933).*

bandages away from his head to reveal nothing – is added the silky-smooth menace of Rains' cultivated voice, sliding into madness as he hatches plans to rule the world.

Universal did not revive the "Invisible Man" cycle until Vincent Price did the disappearing trick to clear himself of a murder charge in **The Invisible Man Returns** (1940). **The Invisible Woman** (1940) was played strictly for laughs, with an aging John Barrymore hamming away bemusedly as the professor who turns fashion model Virginia Bruce transparent. Most of the humor is milked from the possibility that the comely Bruce will rematerialize in a state of undress.

Silken threads
The comedy-thriller **The Invisible Agent** (1942) pitted Jon Hall against the Nazis and the Japanese. At one point Peter Lorre's sinister Oriental spy attempts to snare Hall in a spider's web of transparent silken threads. Hall turned up again in **The Invisible Man's Revenge** (1944), a routine thriller in which he sets out to terrorize the crooks who have framed him. By now Fulton's splendid special effects were merely being used to dress up other-

wise unremarkable B-movies. In similar fashion, science fiction gimmicks were grafted on to the gangster films so popular throughout the 1930s.

In Warners' **The Walking Dead** (1936) Boris Karloff played a man wrongly convicted of murder, executed and then brought back to life by well-meaning scientist Edmund Gwenn. Not surprisingly, Karloff takes a fearful revenge on the real murderers, literally scaring them to death before expiring himself.

An invasion of mad doctors
Karloff was the decade's most accomplished and familiar "mad doctor". No one could match the menacing undertones of his grave and intense screen presence. In Universal's stylish **The Invisible Ray** (1936), which co-starred Bela Lugosi, he played a scientist fatally irradiated with the "Radium X" he has discovered in the African jungle. Lugosi, for once on the side of the angels, develops an antidote, but not before Karloff has become a homicidal maniac. At the end of the decade, he embarked on a series of "mad doctor" roles at Columbia. The first was as **The Man They Could Not Hang** (1939), briskly directed by Nick Grinde, in which Karloff

used a mechanical heart to revive himself after being executed for murder. This was followed by **The Man With Nine Lives** (1940) and **Before I Hang** (1940), both of which blended elements from science fiction and horror films.

More interesting was **The Devil Commands** (1941), efficiently handled by Edward Dmytryk, who later graduated from the B-movie production line to better things. Packing a punch in nearly every one of its 66 minutes of running time, **The Devil Commands** follows Karloff's attempts to communicate with his dead wife by using a machine that registers brain impulses. Predictably the doomed venture ends in tears for all concerned. It also brought the "mad doctor" series to an end.

In 1942 Karloff joined forces with Lorre to send himself up in a slap-happy low-budget comedy, **The Boogie Man Will Get You**, directed by second-feature workhorse Lew Landers. Created as a vehicle to

Below *Bela Lugosi in* **The Invisible Ray** *(1936), directed by Lambert Hillyer and a superior entry in the "mad doctor" cycle of the 1930s.*

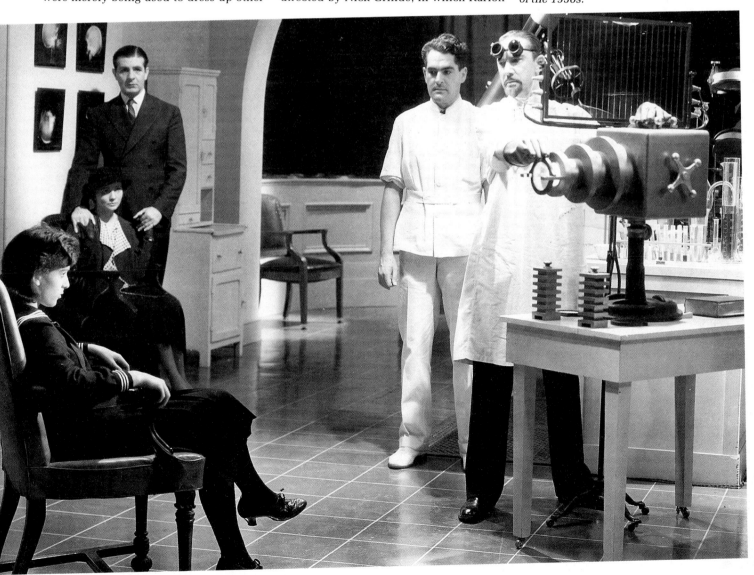

In a pulsating climax, a group of scientists who have been reduced to the size of mice smash his glasses and lure him to his death in the mineshaft that provides him with his source of power. The remarkable shape-changing properties of radioactivity was a theme taken up again in the 1950s, and **Dr. Cyclops** points the way to Jack Arnold's small masterpiece **The Incredible Shrinking Man** (1957).

While big-budget science fiction languished, the flame was kept flickering in Hollywood's Poverty Row and in the studios' B-movie units, where the budgets sometimes threatened to join Jon Hall in their invisibility. Nowhere were they lower than in the serials, where a masked hero or a hooded villain provided a convenient device to keep actors' wages to a minimum.

Fifteen chapters was the classic length of a serial, providing a 20-minute weekly cliffhanger which glued countless children to their Saturday afternoon cinema seats from the silent era to the early 1950s. Frequently they were adapted from comic strips (*Spy Smasher, Flash Gordon, Batman, Superman, Dick Tracy*) or popular radio programmes and pulp fiction (*The Green Hornet, The Shadow, Captain Midnight, The Spider*). They present a child's view of the universe, full of secret passwords, underground hideouts, snarling villains bent on world domination, evil jungle priestesses and chaotic, almost

exploit Karloff's success on Broadway in **Arsenic and Old Lace**, the film finds him trying to build an electrical superman to help the war effort. "Failed again", he mutters peevishly, as another haphazard collection of limbs crashes lifeless from the operating table on to the laboratory floor.

Karloff may have been pre-eminent among cinema's "mad doctors", but he had some notable rivals. In **Mad Love** (1936) Lorre played Dr. Gogol, grafting a murderer's hands on to the mangled arms of concert pianist Clive Brook. Lionel Barrymore was the evil genius of Tod Browning's **The Devil Doll** (1936), escaping from a penal colony and using a secret

Above *The Boogie Man Will Get You (1942), a broad farce in which Boris Karloff tried to turn Maxie Rosenbloom into a superman.*

miniaturization formula as a means of revenge. He plants tiny human assassins in the homes of his enemies and then telepathically orders them on to the attack.

Shrinking victims

A similar theme was taken up in Ernest B. Schoedsack's **Dr. Cyclops** (1940), in which Albert Dekker played the bullet-headed, pebble-spectacled Dr. Thorkel. Hiding out in the Peruvian jungle, he harnesses a radioactive deposit to shrink his victims.

Below *Colin Clive and Peter Lorre in **Mad Love** (1936) directed by the German cinematographer Karl Freund.*

dream-like violence and action.

In Mascot's **Phantom Empire** (1935), an early starring vehicle for Gene Autry, the yodelling cowpoke spends his time galloping between "Radio Ranch" and Murania, a bizarre underground civilization located at the bottom of a disused mineshaft. This low-budget version of **Things to Come** is awash with robots, ray guns, posses and frequent bouts of warbling from Autry. It remains one of the curiosities of cinema, a remarkable blend of horse opera and science fiction.

"Crash" Corrigan

Soon after the release of **Phantom Empire**, Mascot was absorbed by Republic, who immediately rushed out **Undersea Kingdom** (1936), in which cowboy hero Ray "Crash" Corrigan uses a rocket-powered submarine to rediscover the lost city of Atlantis. Again, audiences were treated to a range of scientific gadgetry which sits alongside the serial's furious swordfights and pseudo-Roman costumes.

Right *Humphrey Bogart in* **The Return of Dr. X** *(1939).*
Below *The evil Dr. Thorkel (Albert Dekker) and his miniaturized victims in* **Dr. Cyclops** *(1940). It was directed by Ernest B. Schoedsack, besk known for his production of the fantasy classic* **King Kong** *(1933).*
Bottom *Lobby card for Tod Browning's* **Devil Doll** *(1936).*

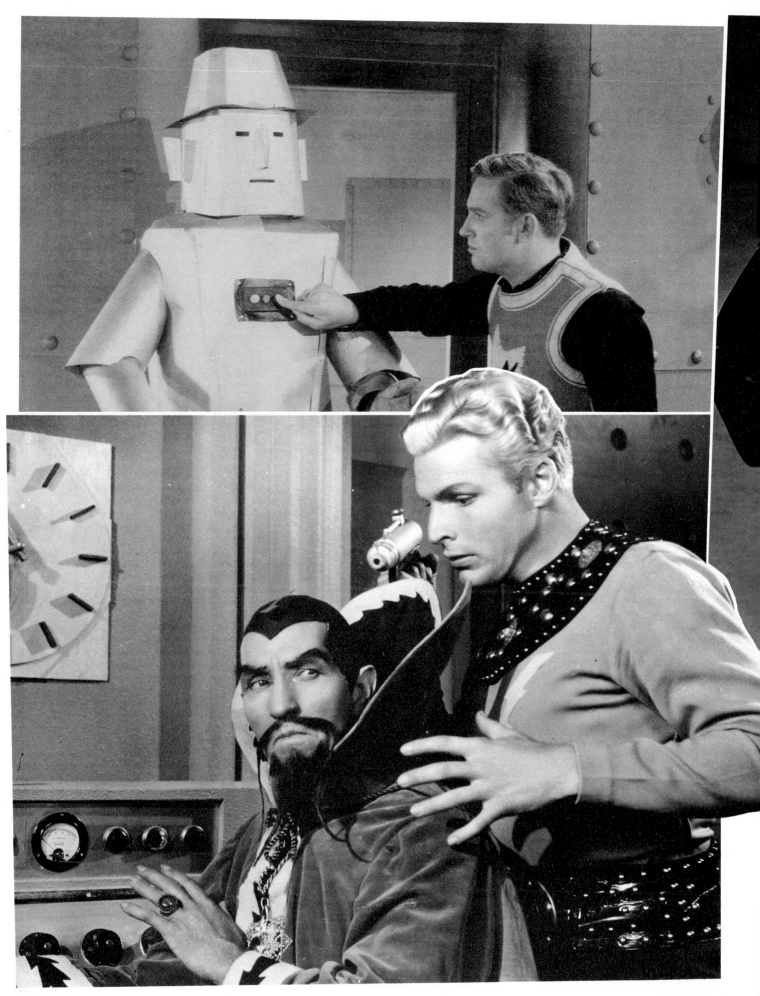

Above left *Clearly missing his ten-gallon hat, frozen-faced cowpoke Gene Autry tangles with a cardboard robot in the Mascot serial **Phantom Empire** (1935).* **Left** *Flash Gordon (Buster Crabbe) catches up with Ming the Merciless (Charles Middleton) in episode seven of **Flash Gordon's Trip to Mars** (1938).* **Above** *Buster Crabbe and Constance Moore find trouble in **Buck Rogers** (1939).*

Vying with **Undersea Kingdom** was Universal's **Flash Gordon** (1936), the most enduring of the decade's science fiction serials. Based on Alex Raymond's superbly drawn comic strip, it starred Buster Crabbe as the blond, firm-jawed hero battling Lion Men, Shark Men and Giant Orangapoids in his crusade against Ming the Merciless, tyrant of the gypsy planet Mongo.

Universal made two more Flash Gordon serials: **Flash Gordon's Trip to Mars** (1938), which was inspired by Orson Welles' celebrated radio version of *The War of the Worlds*, and **Flash Gordon Conquers the Universe** (1940). While they never captured the elegant draughtsmanship of Raymond's comic strip, they did succeed in creating the self-contained world that is the basis of all fantasy. Along the way they displayed a disarmingly cock-eyed flexibility, borrowing elements from Nordic and Anglo-Saxon mythology, sets and costumes from other films, ray guns and Roman armor, in a fantastical universe that still retains much of its original charm. Running through the middle of the serial was a complicated romantic and sexual tangle in which the evil Ming lusts after Flash's beautiful companion Dale Arden, while his own daughter, the voluptuous Aura, has the hots for Flash.

Against a backdrop of sputtering rockets moving jerkily across the screen on their wires, papier-mâché caverns and cost-conscious armies of extras, unlikely helmets jammed unsteadily on their heads, the principal characters in **Flash Gordon** remain locked in an endless embrace.

Following this success, Universal cast Buster Crabbe as Buck Rogers, the hero of America's first science fiction comic strip. In **Buck Rogers** (1939), Crabbe wakes up to

find himself in the twenty-fifth century and pitted against Killer Kane and the evil Captain Lasca, the latter part played to the hilt by Henry Brandon, one of the great serial villains. **Buck Rogers** tried hard to capture the flavor of the original **Flash Gordon**, but, despite some newly designed rockets and Brandon's cultivated villainy, the serial degenerated into a series of hectic chases and dull dialogue sequences.

Fiendish gadgetry

No serial was complete without a criminal mastermind drooling over a piece of fiendish gadgetry calculated to blow us all to oblivion. In the **Mysterious Dr. Satan** (1940), Eduardo Ciannelli builds a robot army but is called to task by the masked hero, "Copperhead". His sardine-can robot

Above *Harry Worth as "The Scorpion" in* **The Adventures of Captain Marvel** *(1941).* **Below** *The Martian invader in* **The Purple Monster Strikes** *(1945).*

– the sole representative of his mighty army – had first been used in **Undersea Kingdom** and turned up 12 years later in **Zombies of the Stratosphere** (1952).

In Republic's **The Adventures of Captain Marvel** (1941), the hooded Scorpion's atom-smashing device threatens freedom, democracy and everything we hold dear. In the same studio's **The Crimson Ghost** (1946), lurking behind a death's head mask, plans to turn his deadly cyclotrode on Earth's helpless population. To make his task easier he develops a "control collar" which, placed around his victims' necks, reduces them to zombies. In **Dick Tracy vs Crime Inc** (1941), also Republic, the Ghost uses a weird contraption to make himself invisible. Jut-jawed hero Tracy ensures that the Ghost comes to a sticky end, frying him to a crisp on some high-tension power cables. Perhaps the most beguiling mastermind of them all was the Lightning who, in Republic's **Fighting Devil Dogs** (1938), unleashes a devastating thunderbolt machine against the US Marines. His inevitable death in the final reel leaves one with a real sense of loss.

Right *Superman was first played on screen by Kirk Alyn in 1948. Christopher Reeve assumed the role in* **Superman – The Movie** *(1978). Here he grapples with the evil Zod (Terence Stamp) in* **Superman II** *(1980).*
Below *The masked Copperhead (Robert Wilcox) in* **Mysterious Dr. Satan** *(1940).*

CHAPTER THREE

The Golden Age Of The 1950s

G-Men battling crazed masterminds armed with death rays, po-faced cowboys disarming cardboard robots, and the comic consequences of invisibility were the stock-in-trade of science fiction cinema in the 1940s. But the real world was about to burst in. While the caped crusader Batman took on the zombie army controlled by J. Carrol Naish's sinister Dr. Daka, the men behind the Manhattan project were working steadily towards a weapon which would make the Crimson Ghost's deadly cyclot-rode look like a pop-gun.

In **Batman** (1943), Dr. Daka was out to steal America's radium for the Axis powers, and it was in the field of nuclear physics that the breakthrough came that irrevocably changed the world in which we live. Science had set free a force so frightening that it was possible to contemplate the extinction of our own species.

At the same time, the development of the V2 rocket in Germany had provided the platform from which man would eventually launch himself into space. On the one hand science had brought us to the threshold of the space age while at the same time holding out the seemingly limitless possibilities and benefits of nuclear power; on the other hand lay the possibility of annihilation. The Cold War cast long shadows over a world so recently saved for democracy.

Far left *Osa Massen and Lloyd Bridges hurtle towards Mars in* **Rocketship X-M** *(1950).* **Left** *The impressive set built for* **Destination Moon** *(1950), which marked the arrival of documentary realism in science fiction cinema.* **Below** *The immovable robot Gort from* **The Day the Earth Stood Still** *(1951).*

Above *The Thing* (1951), which created a sharp division between fans of science fiction literature and science fiction cinema.

In the United States, fear of the Soviet Union, and fear of subversion from within, led to a climate of paranoia which was reflected in the witch-hunt against suspected Communists led by Senator Joseph McCarthy. Underneath the bland, materialistic surface of Eisenhower's America,

fierce currents swirled to and fro. Many of them were channelled into the science fiction film, the perfect vehicle for expressing the tensions of the age.

Moon shots

Paradoxically, the film that launched the 1950s science fiction boom, George Pal's **Destination Moon** (1950), was a sober, documentary-influenced celebration of man's imminent conquest of space. Adapted from Robert Heinlein's pulp novel *Rocketship Galileo*, **Destination Moon** concentrated on realism and detail at the expense of drama. Hermann Oberth, who had advised Fritz Lang on the making of **Die Frau im Mond** (**The Woman in the Moon**, 1929), was called in as the rocketry consultant. It took a hundred men nearly two months to build the cratered moonscape designed by Ernst Figte. Nevertheless, there is a hint of the Cold War in a US General's remark that "if the United States doesn't get to the Moon first, someone else will".

Destination Moon was a big commercial success, scooping the 1950 Oscar for special effects. While it was still in production a rush-released low-budget imitation, Kurt Neumann's **Rocketship X-M**, was playing in American cinemas. Once again the Moon was the target, but the rocket veers off course, depositing its crew on

Below *John Carpenter's 1982 remake of* **The Thing,** *which stuck closely to the original story and boasted some spectacular special effects.*

Mars. Here they find the impressive remains of a technologically advanced civilization apparently destroyed in a nuclear holocaust. After being attacked by some surviving Martians – blind Stone Age primitives – the rocket returns to Earth where, in a surprisingly downbeat ending, it crashes, killing all the survivors of the expedition.

Watch the skies!

The success of **Destination Moon** had reawakened the major studios' interest in science fiction. Fox and RKO put into production two big-budget features aimed at expanding the bridgehead shrewdly established by the independent Pal. Both of them reversed Pal's image of man reaching out to the stars. In Fox's **The Day the Earth Stood Still** (1951) and RKO's **The Thing** (1951), Earth, in its turn, is visited by beings from outer space.

The Day the Earth Stood Still was adapted from Harry Bates' story *Farewell to the Master* and directed by Robert Wise. Among the best science fiction films of the decade, it contains one of the most haunting images of the 1950s – a giant silver flying saucer descending on a baseball diamond in a park in the middle of Washington. It brings with it an austere, lofty, humanoid alien, Klaatu (Michael Rennie), and his massive robot Gort, whose heat ray turns the US Army's artillery and tanks into piles of smouldering scrap. Klaatu has been despatched by an alien planetary federation to warn Earthlings to cease developing and testing nuclear weapons.

In an attempt to find out what human beings are really like, Klaatu, incognito, moves into a small boarding-house and strikes up a credible relationship with its owner (Patricia Neal) and her small son. Not all humans are so accommodating, however, and Klaatu is shot dead by a jittery soldier. Christlike, he is brought back to life by Gort before ascending into the heavens. He leaves Gort behind in charge of a robot police force. If Earth's inhabitants cannot live in peace with each other, they will invite their own destruction – rather a violent parting message from the emissary of a peace-loving intergalactic federation.

This benevolent but slightly sinister authoritarianism is in sharp contrast to the rampaging monster on the loose at the center of **The Thing**. Nominally directed by Christian Nyby, **The Thing** was in fact closely supervised by its producer Howard Hawks – and bears his stamp.

In another of the great set pieces in science fiction cinema, the staff of an American scientific base in the Arctic discover a crashed UFO. As a blizzard races towards them across the horizon they space themselves out in a circle across the ice, indicating the size of the aliens' craft. The hardbitten Air Force officer (Kenneth Tobey) – the archetypal Hawksian man of action – who has been

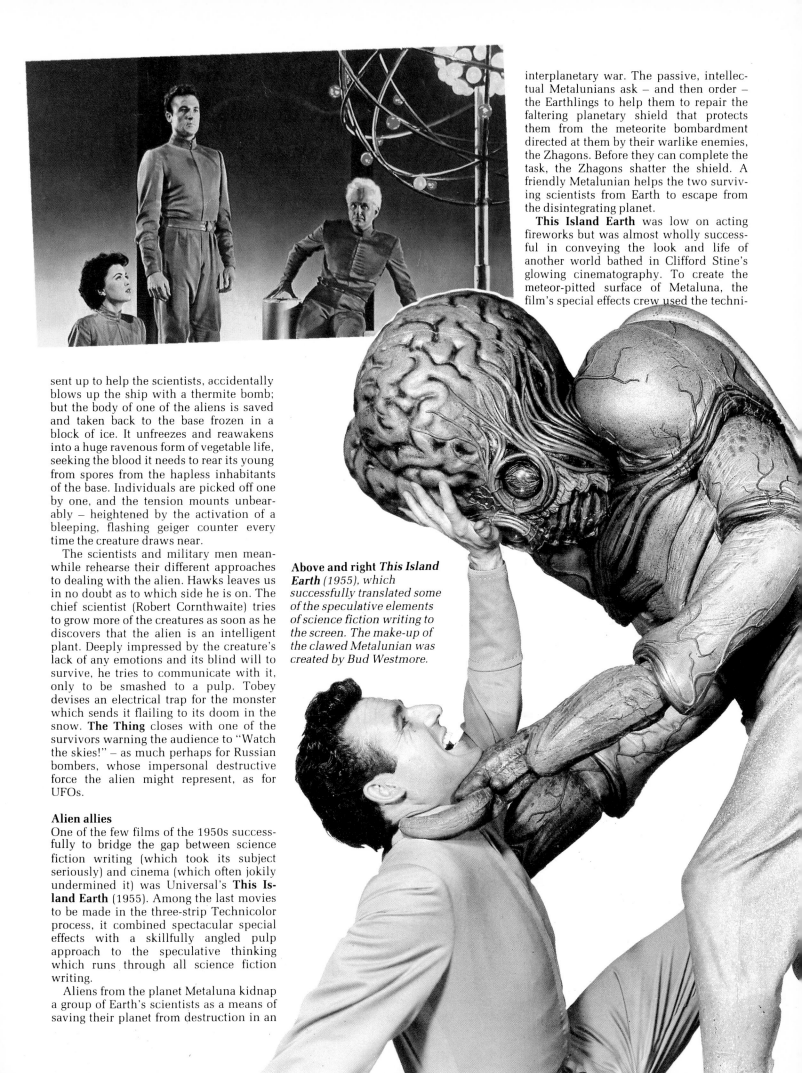

interplanetary war. The passive, intellectual Metalunians ask – and then order – the Earthlings to help them to repair the faltering planetary shield that protects them from the meteorite bombardment directed at them by their warlike enemies, the Zhagons. Before they can complete the task, the Zhagons shatter the shield. A friendly Metalunian helps the two surviving scientists from Earth to escape from the disintegrating planet.

This Island Earth was low on acting fireworks but was almost wholly successful in conveying the look and life of another world bathed in Clifford Stine's glowing cinematography. To create the meteor-pitted surface of Metaluna, the film's special effects crew used the techni-

sent up to help the scientists, accidentally blows up the ship with a thermite bomb; but the body of one of the aliens is saved and taken back to the base frozen in a block of ice. It unfreezes and reawakens into a huge ravenous form of vegetable life, seeking the blood it needs to rear its young from spores from the hapless inhabitants of the base. Individuals are picked off one by one, and the tension mounts unbearably – heightened by the activation of a bleeping, flashing geiger counter every time the creature draws near.

The scientists and military men meanwhile rehearse their different approaches to dealing with the alien. Hawks leaves us in no doubt as to which side he is on. The chief scientist (Robert Cornthwaite) tries to grow more of the creatures as soon as he discovers that the alien is an intelligent plant. Deeply impressed by the creature's lack of any emotions and its blind will to survive, he tries to communicate with it, only to be smashed to a pulp. Tobey devises an electrical trap for the monster which sends it flailing to its doom in the snow. **The Thing** closes with one of the survivors warning the audience to "Watch the skies!" – as much perhaps for Russian bombers, whose impersonal destructive force the alien might represent, as for UFOs.

Above and right *This Island Earth (1955), which successfully translated some of the speculative elements of science fiction writing to the screen. The make-up of the clawed Metalunian was created by Bud Westmore.*

Alien allies
One of the few films of the 1950s successfully to bridge the gap between science fiction writing (which took its subject seriously) and cinema (which often jokily undermined it) was Universal's **This Island Earth** (1955). Among the last movies to be made in the three-strip Technicolor process, it combined spectacular special effects with a skillfully angled pulp approach to the speculative thinking which runs through all science fiction writing.

Aliens from the planet Metaluna kidnap a group of Earth's scientists as a means of saving their planet from destruction in an ques pioneered in **Metropolis**, building a detailed model 110 feet long. The miniature meteors were magnesium encased in plaster. They were shot along wires to the model's surface, where electrical charges were set to ignite gasoline for the blinding white explosions caused by impact.

This Island Earth was followed by MGM's only major excursion into science fiction in the 1950s, **Forbidden Planet** (1956). An updated version of *The Tempest*, it cast Walter Pidgeon as the Prospero figure, a scientist called Morbius who lives with his daughter Alta (Anne Francis) on the planet Altair IV. Like *The*

Tempest's Miranda, Alta has never seen any man but her father. The role of Ariel is filled by the film's most charming character, Robbie the Robot, a seven-foot mechanical wonder who is equally at home neutralizing weapons, manufacturing booze and precious gems to order, or smugly exchanging humorless small-talk with other members of the cast.

Target Earth

Despite their superb production values and imaginative special effects, both **This Island Earth** and **Forbidden Planet** were financial failures. **Forbidden Planet** cost

well over a million dollars to make, but the receipts came to little more than $1,600,000. A low-budget film released in the same year, **Earth Versus the Flying Saucers** (1956), took in almost as much at the box-office.

Earth Versus the Flying Saucers, with its dreamlike stop-motion photography by Ray Harryhausen, brings us back to the threat posed by alien visitors. At times it must have seemed as if the skies above America were black with spacecraft, all lining up to disgorge hostile crews armed with invincible weaponry, but usually afflicted with an unlikely Achilles heel

Right *Robby the Robot, the most engaging character in* **Forbidden Planet** *(1956). Robby was operated from the inside by pint-sized actor Frankie Darro whose face was blackened to keep it invisible behind the neon grating in Robby's chest.*

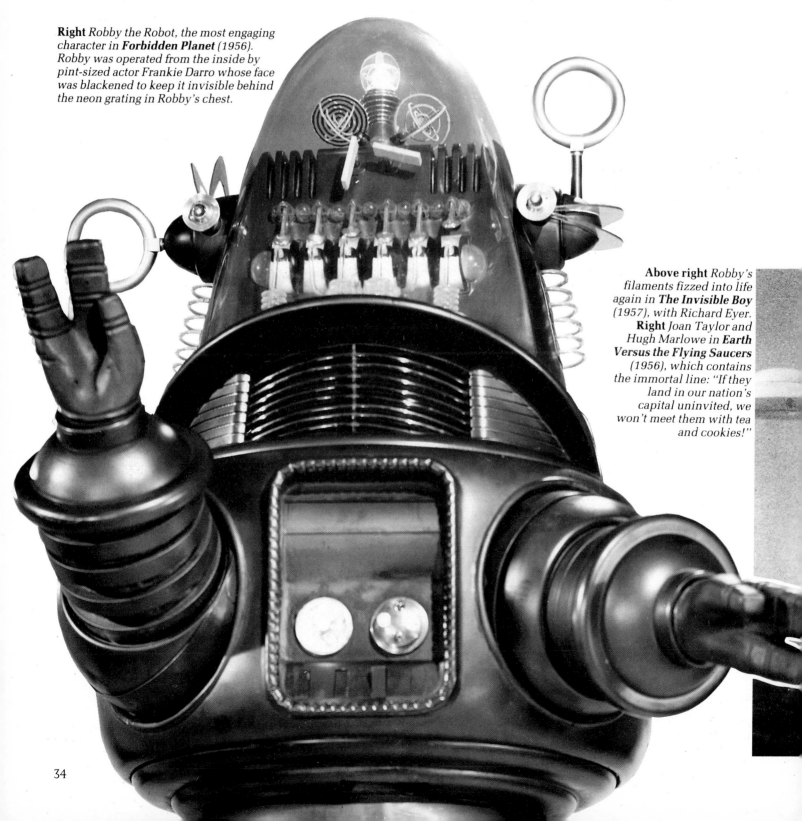

Above right *Robby's filaments fizzed into life again in* **The Invisible Boy** *(1957), with Richard Eyer.* **Right** *Joan Taylor and Hugh Marlowe in* **Earth Versus the Flying Saucers** *(1956), which contains the immortal line: "If they land in our nation's capital uninvited, we won't meet them with tea and cookies!"*

vastating heat rays, combining impersonal streamlined technology with an image of bestial violence. They remain unmoved by the man of God who advances towards them reciting the 23rd Psalm, Bible held high, its cross glinting bravely in the pulsing glow thrown off by their craft. He is incinerated by the Martians, who then turn their attentions to the chillingly clinical destruction of Los Angeles. In the end God has his way: the Martians die, felled by common or garden bacteria.

A long way from home
War of the Worlds and **Earth Versus the Flying Saucers** featured mass invasions of our planet. In Roger Corman's inventive **Not of This Earth** (1956), the alien threat was embodied by gravel-voiced Paul Birch in a business suit and a pair of dark glasses. Removing the shades, he reveals a pair of ping-pong eyeballs that scramble his victims' brains. Whipping a transfusion kit from his briefcase, he drains their blood, which is despatched by matter transmitter to the irradiated population of the planet Davana. Like the central characters in a number of Corman's later films – notably Ray Milland in **The Man With X-Ray Eyes** (1963) – Birch is a powerful but ultimately rarefied creature, unable to withstand extremes of noise and driven to his doom by the wailing of the klaxon on a

that brings about their destruction. Scientist Hugh Marlowe discovers that the aliens are sensitive to high-frequency sound. Beamed up at their spacecraft, it causes them to plunge spectacularly into a number of famous Washington landmarks.

Ironically, the leathery aliens, voyaging from their dying planet, are not initially hostile to mankind. They only turn nasty when the boneheaded Earthlings greet them with gunfire. This was a fate also suffered by the lonely alien in Edgar

Ulmer's **The Man From Planet X** (1951), who finds his welcome on Earth as cold as the climate on his own doomed, freezing planet.

There was no doubt, however, about the intentions of the Martian invaders in George Pal's **War of the Worlds** (1953), an updated version of Wells' novel set in California. The sleek, menacing Martian war machines glide across the landscape like giant Manta rays. Their slender, swivelling, cobra-like necks spit out de-

Above *Predatory Martian war machines glide across the Californian landscape in George Pal's* **War of the Worlds** *(1953).*

police motorcycle. At the end of the film the camera pans up to a tombstone that reads "Here Lies a Man Who Was Not of This Earth", then pulls away to reveal another menacing figure in black suit and dark glasses plodding towards us.

The anti-hero of **Kronos** (1957), a 100-foot-high alien robot, is after not our blood but our energy. Arriving on a California beach, it lumbers inland, gorging itself on "food" from the power stations in its path. It gobbles up an H-bomb like a performing seal at feeding time, emerging from the blast larger than ever. Finally Jeff Morrow disposes of this intergalactic version of the Juggernaut by shortcircuiting it into absorbing its own accumulated energy. In spite of its painfully limited budget, **Kronos'** special effects are surprisingly convincing.

Special effects are almost subliminal in Corman's **It Conquered the World** (1956), in which idealistic Lee Van Cleef plays host to a cucumber-shaped, fanged Venusian.

However in David Kramarsky's **The Beast With a Million Eyes** (1956), the special effects were virtually dispensed with – a common hazard in a field of filmmaking where the movie was often built around a sensational title. The Beast in question is an economically invisible telepathic alien force that impels birds, cattle and domestic animals to turn on the nearest available human. This Z-grade metaphor for a malevolent God looks forward to Alfred Hitchcock's **The Birds** (1963) and the "revenge of nature" films of the 1970s, when the popular concern with ecology provided science fiction filmmakers with a new area to explore.

The Beast With a Million Eyes looks like a masterpiece when set against **Robot Monster** (1953), whose menace from the outer galaxies, the Ro-Man, was bit-part actor George Barrows in a moth-eaten gorilla suit with a diver's helmet rammed on his head. There are few sights as endearingly absurd in science fiction cinema as that of the dreaded Ro-Man flailing his shaggy arms to activate the deadly Calcinator Death Ray.

Invisible invaders

At least the Ro-Man was visible to the six surviving Earthlings he was bent on destroying. A more insidious threat was posed by aliens who took possession of human bodies and became the "enemy

Below *The last resting place for the lonely alien invader in Roger Corman's exuberantly inventive low-budget* **Not of This Earth** *(1956).* **Right** *Ray Milland as the tortured Dr. Xavier in* **The Man With X-Ray Eyes** *(1963).*

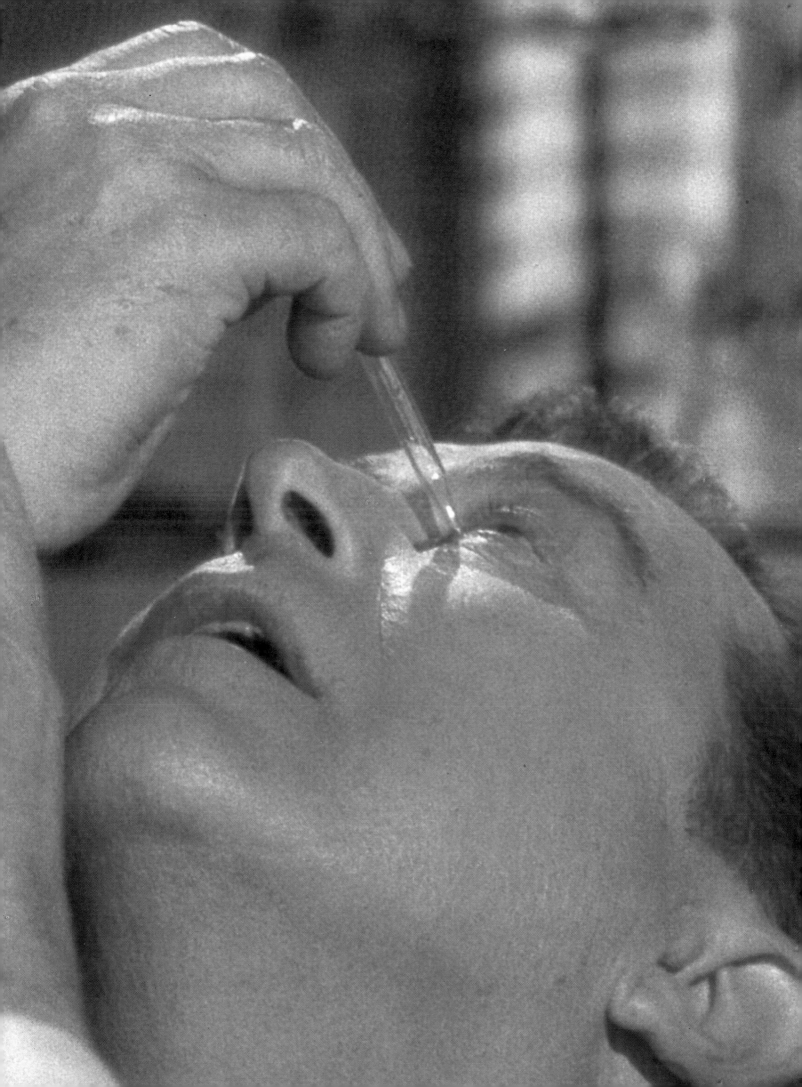

within", indistinguishable from the rest of humanity. This theme touches closely on the postwar American fear of Communist subversion and of Reds lurking under the virtuous beds of Middle America. It prompted a cycle of films that began with William Cameron Menzies' **Invaders From Mars** (1953).

A small boy is woken at night by a flying saucer that lands behind his house and buries itself beneath the sandpit in the backyard. When his genial scientist father (Leif Erickson) goes to investigate he is sucked down through the sand and returned as an irascible automaton with a strange device planted in the back of his neck. Mom quickly goes the same way, as does little Nancy from next door, the police chief and the military head of a nearby rocket development base where the boy's father is a scientist.

The transformation of the child's parents into hard-faced automata – a universal neurosis of childhood – is cleverly handled. The point of view is that of the small boy, and the nightmare quality is heightened by the skillful use of oversized sets and startlingly composed shots. Eventually an astronomer believes the boy's tale and the full might of the US Army is turned on the aliens – an early example of the "total mobilization" methods employed against an extraterrestrial threat.

Sadly, the producers' insistence on endless stock footage of rumbling tank columns on the move clashes horribly with Menzies' small but elegantly contrived studio set of the sandpit in the backyard that hides the Martian invaders.

In Jack Arnold's atmospheric **It Came From Outer Space** (1953), one of the first big 3-D movies, a huge, meteor-like spacecraft lands in the desert near a small Arizona town. Arnold uses the bleak, haunting menace of the setting to good effect as the visitors set about replacing increasing numbers of the town's population with alien doubles. They are identical to their originals, but a series of skillfully planted touches indicates their "otherness". In one brilliant moment, two truck drivers who have been taken over emerge from a darkened alley, holding hands to

Below *Beverly Garland is alarmed by Richard Crane's skin condition in* **Alligator People** *(1959).* **Right** *Richard Carlson is dwarfed by the alien spacecraft in* **It Came From Outer Space** *(1953).* **Inset** *The alien menace in* **It! The Terror From Beyond Space** *(1958).*

reassure each other. But one of them stares, steadily and unblinkingly, into the brutal glare of the noonday sun.

The aliens mean no harm. They merely need mechanics to help them to repair their damaged spaceship. They take a local astronomer (Richard Carlson) into their confidence and at the film's climax he heads off the forces intent on destroying the aliens before they take their leave of Earth.

Pod perfect

The most celebrated of all films to deal with the theme of alien possession is Don Siegel's **Invasion of the Body Snatchers** (1956), in which the inhabitants of a sleepy California town are remorselessly replaced by automaton-like simulacra

hatched from enormous seed pods. At the center of the film is the chilling mystery of the process of the takeover. The doctor hero (Kevin McCarthy), who is already alarmed by the strange behavior of his patients, is shown a "blank" pod lying on the pool table of a close friend. As soon as the friend closes his eyes in sleep the "pod person" will replace him. McCarthy finds replacements for himself and his girlfriend (Dana Wynter) in his greenhouse. In a gruesome sequence he takes a pitchfork to his own incomplete image as it bursts obscenely from an oozing pod, but cannot bring himself to mutilate his girlfriend's replacement, so close is its resemblance to humanity. Inevitably, the girl succumbs to sleep and the possession of the alien intelligence. By now McCarthy's despera-

Above right *Radioactive primeval slime threatens the world in the British* **X – The Unknown** *(1956).* **Right** *Astronaut Richard Wordsworth invaded by a malevolent alien vegetable in* **The Quatermass Experiment** *(1955).*

tion is multiplied as the good citizens of Santa Maria have begun to despatch the pods all over America. In the film's memorable closing image, he stumbles along a freeway yelling "You're next!" to the faceless and uncomprehending drivers flashing past him.

Invasion of the Body Snatchers has been cited both as a classic anti-McCarthy tract and as a distillation of 1950s anti-Communist paranoia. While it is possible to interpret the film along either of these lines, its real concern seems to be with the mysterious borderline between human emotions and the behavior of automata. At the kernel of the movie is a short, disturbing scene in which a nurse, already taken over by the aliens, decides that a pod should be placed in a small baby's cot, as then "there will be no more crying".

Cold War frenzy

A number of science fiction films of the 1950s tackled the supposed Communist threat head-on, often with engagingly weird results. In **Red Planet Mars** (1952), clean-cut scientist Peter Graves discovers that God is broadcasting to us from Mars. A crazed, drink-sodden scientist – a former Nazi now in the pay of the Russians – turns up to declare that he is responsible for all the uplifting messages. Graves solves the problem by blowing himself, the Communist and his young wife to

Right *Sexual politics mingle with science fiction in* **I Married a Monster From Outer Space** *(1958).* **Below** *Donald Sutherland's alien replicant in the remake of* **Invasion of the Body Snatchers** *(1978).*

Above *Ralph Meeker (center) as Mickey Spillane's Mike Hammer in Robert Aldrich's blistering* **Kiss Me Deadly** *(1955).* **Right** *The usual mayhem breaks out in* **Godzilla Versus the Bionic Monster** *(1974), in which Godzilla takes on a replicant robot controlled by alien invaders.* **Far right** *Astral triffids on the rampage in* **The Green Slime** *(1968).*

smithereens in his laboratory – but not before a final message comes over the line, "Well done, thou good and faithful servant."

A combination of Nazism and Communism also featured in William Cameron Menzies' **The Whip Hand** (1951), in which a former Nazi germ warfare expert plans to make the world safe for Communism by releasing plague bacilli into America's water supply. In a climax reminiscent of **The Island of Lost Souls** (1932), he is beaten to death by his own grotesque human guinea pigs.

From the frantic convolutions of films like **The Whip Hand** it was a short step to the contemplation of nuclear war. First into the field was Arch Oboler's **Five** (1951), in which five brawling survivors of the holocaust inhabit a deserted world. **Five** influenced Alfred E. Green's **Invasion USA** (1952) in which Dan O'Herlihy is a mysterious stranger hypnotizing a group of people in a New York bar into believing that the Soviet Union launched an all-out nuclear attack.

Atomic disaster overtook California in Robert Aldrich's breathless Micky Spillane adaptation **Kiss Me Deadly** (1955), when a Pandora's box of radioactive material is opened, explodes and ushers in the apocalypse. In **The World, the Flesh and the Devil** (1959), the apocalypse has left New York with just three inhabitants – Harry Belafonte, Mel Ferrer and Inger Stevens – who act out a clumsy morality play in the city's empty streets and echoing buildings. Equally clumsy was Stanley Kramer's **On the Beach** (1959), in which Australia waits for the arrival of the fall-out that has already destroyed the rest of the world.

Burdened with a starry cast – Gregory Peck, Fred Astaire and Ava Gardner – the issue of the aftermath of nuclear war is buried under the weight of personal melodramas: submarine captain Peck's doomed affair with cynical socialite Gardner; racing driver Astaire's decision to gas himself with the fumes from the exhaust of his sports car rather than swallow the death capsules handed out by the government.

Ray Milland's low-budget **Panic in the Year Zero** (1962) took a more direct line. Fleeing into the hills with his family after a Soviet pre-emptive strike flattens Los Angeles, Milland reveals himself as a survivor *par excellence*, refusing shelter to weaker souls and shooting down in cold blood the hoodlums who rape his daughter. The ironies implicit in making preparations to survive a nuclear war ran through Joseph Losey's **The Damned** (1961), in which Alexander Knox presides over an eerie brood of deliberately irradiated children with whom he can only communicate by television. If the bomb drops the children will live on in a world in which their silver-suited protectors will not survive.

Also planning to survive is Peter Sellers' ex-Nazi scientist Dr Strangelove, the twitching, black-gloved descendant of Rotwang who advises the US President in

Out of primordial depths to destroy the world!

COLUMBIA
PICTURES
presents

IT CAME FROM BENEATH THE SEA

starring
KENNETH TOBEY
FAITH DOMERGUE
with DONALD CURTIS

Copyright 1955 Columbia Pictures Corp.

PRINTED IN U. S. A.

Above *Ray Harryhausen's low-budget sea monster rises from the deep to destroy the Golden Gate Bridge in* **It Came From Beneath the Sea** *(1955), one of the year's surprise money-makers.*

Stanley Kubrick's apocalyptic black comedy **Dr. Strangelove or How I Learned to Stop Worrying and Love the Bomb** (1964). For Strangelove, squirming ecstatically in his wheelchair, the descent towards chaos – triggered by a demented US general's belief that the Reds are draining "our vital bodily fluids" – is the ultimate turn-on. In **Strangelove**, Kubrick orchestrates two related fears: on a human level, those who are in a position to prevent a nuclear war

are also who are most drawn towards it; and on a technological level, represented by the Russian "Doomsday Machine", we have mortgaged our future to buy machines we cannot control.

Godzilla

The Japanese have already experienced the shattering consequences of nuclear attack, and since 1945 they have remained understandably sensitive about all things nuclear. The possibility of monstrous side-effects stemming from nuclear accident is the theme that dominates the Toho Studio's long series of monster epics, the first of which was **Godzilla, King of the Monsters** (1954). A 400-foot *Tyrannosaurus Rex* raised from the deep by an

atom-bomb test at Bikini Atoll, Godzilla shrugs off atomic depth charges and other puny human attempts to impede his progress, and heads for Tokyo.

As he goes he breathes a deadly radioactive fire, topples skyscrapers, rips up trains and high-voltage power lines, and generally does everything that comes naturally to an oversized killer dinosaur.

Drastic measures are taken to destroy him, including an attempt to drain the oxygen from the Pacific. They are not drastic enough, however, as Godzilla returned in a steady stream of follow-ups, including **Godzilla's Counterattack** (1955), **Godzilla Versus the Thing** (1964) and **Son of Godzilla** (1966). In an increasingly ritualistic attempt to exorcise

44

radiation run through all the Toho films. Even in **Frankenstein Conquers the World** (1966) the monster of the title is a human who has grown to colossal size after feasting on the irradiated heart of Frankenstein's monster. In the 1960s the series came to a climax with **Destroy All Monsters** (1968); all the Toho monsters have been imprisoned on an island (a metaphor for nuclear disarmament) before escaping from under the control of alien invaders and going on the rampage.

Creature features

In Jack Arnold's **The Creature From the Black Lagoon** (1954), another monster rose from the depths to win a place in popular mythology. Half-man, half-fish, the Gill-Man discovered by Richard Denning's expedition is as threatening as the ravenous Great White shark in **Jaws** (1975), over which it exercised a considerable influence. The long, erotic underwater sequence in which the Creature swims below Julia Adams, mimicking the languorous movements of her body, was lifted by Steven Spielberg for the opening of **Jaws**, a debt that this modern "movie brat" was quick to acknowledge.

Jack Arnold said of his creature, "It plays upon a basic fear that people have about what might be lurking below the surface of any body of water. You know the feeling when you are swimming and something brushes your legs down below – it scares the hell out of you if you don't know what it is. It's the fear of the unknown."

Taking a leaf out of the Toho book, film makers turned to the A-bomb tests as a dramatic mechanism for awakening monsters from their primeval slumbers. In **The Beast From 20,000 Fathoms** (1953), their reverberations interrupted the hibernation

of a dinosaur frozen in the arctic ice. The creature returns to its ancestral home – which is now covered by New York – where it meets a fiery end, trapped in the roller coasters of Coney Island. The giant octopus that Ray Harryhausen created for **It Came From Beneath the Sea** (1955) was in fact a pentapus, as the slender budget led Harryhausen to the shrewd conclusion that five arms were cheaper to animate than eight. Despite this handicap the animal performed a smart demolition job on the Golden Gate Bridge before being killed with a nuclear-armed torpedo.

Atom tests in the Nevada desert nourished a race of monster ants in Gordon Douglas' **Them!** (1954). They invade the sewers of Los Angeles where they are burnt alive in a catacomb of storm drains. **Them!** was an enormous box-office success, prompting a swarm of imitators. In **Tarantula** (1955), a giant spider lumbered out of the Arizona desert. The by-product of Leo G. Carroll's experiments in

the ghost of Hiroshima, the Toho special effects department created a complete monster iconography, including Ghidrah the three-headed dragon; Rodan, a vast pterodactyl; and Dogora, a giant jellyfish from outer space.

The twin themes of atomic war and

*__Above right__ Julia Adams meets **The Creature From the Black Lagoon** (1954). Out of the water he was played by Ben Chapman and underwater by Ricou Browning. Sequels were **Revenge of the Creature** (1955) and **The Creature Walks Among Us** (1956). **Right** End of the line for **The Deadly Mantis** (1957), zapped in an underground parking lot.*

Inset left *Leo G. Carroll in* **Tarantula** *(1955), one of the off-shoots of* **Them!** *(1954).* **Inset right** *Glenn Langan growing at the rate of 10 feet a day in* **The Amazing Colossal Man** *(1957).* **Left** *Lily Tomlin gets an accidental dose of a new perfume – "Sexpot" – that sends her in the opposite direction in* **The Incredible Shrinking Woman** *(1981), a limp feminist comedy loosely derived from* **The Incredible Shrinking Man** *(1957).*

"accelerated tissue growth", the overgrown arachnid received the King Kong treatment at the hands of the US Air Force, although its nemesis was now a jet interceptor armed with napalm rather than a biplane. The installation of an early warning system near the North Pole disturbs **The Deadly Mantis** (1957), a 200-foot-long insect that wings its way south, creating havoc along America's eastern seaboard. It is finally cornered and destroyed in that classic no-man's-land of the American urban thriller, an underground parking lot.

Ups and downs
The effects of radiation on human beings were, on the whole, equally straightforward. They made you either very big or very small. In Jack Arnold's **The Incredible Shrinking Man** (1957), a radioactive cloud has an alarming effect on Grant Williams. As he diminishes his paranoia increases. As he shrinks to midget size his wife looms threateningly over him. Smaller still, he becomes the prey of the family cat who prowls around the doll's house in which he is forced to live. Falling unnoticed into the basement, he does battle with a spider which, to him, is the size of the monster insect in Arnold's **Tarantula**. Finally he slips through the mesh grating in the cellar window and into the garden. Dwarfed by the blades of grass, as the film ends he is on the point of sliding away into the infinity of nothingness.

In Bert I. Gordon's **The Amazing Col-ossal Man** (1957), Glenn Langan took a journey in the opposite direction. Accidentally contaminated during an A-bomb test in the desert, he begins to grow at the rate of 10 feet a day. Soon his home is a circus tent, a pointed reminder of his freakishness. Driven mad with anguish, he descends on Las Vegas, stumbling past huge neon signs his own size and pursued by a scientific team armed with a monster syringe filled with shrinking serum. After a few half-hearted jabs at a big papiermâché ankle, they are forced to stand by helplessly as a GI shoots the unhappy giant off Boulder Dam with a bazooka.

In Fred Sears' **The Werewolf** (1956), Steve Ritch turns into a Wolf Man after scientists inject him with a serum to combat radiation poisoning. In similar fashion, atom experiments transform John Beal into a bloodsucker in **The Vampire** (1957). These films mark the point at which the dormant horror genre began to reassert itself over the flagging science fiction film. Hammer released **The Curse of Frankenstein** (1957) in the same year as **The Vampire**.

Another indication that the science fiction boom was burning itself out was seen in the increasingly frantic efforts by exploitation producers to graft the science fiction movie on to the "teen agony" and biker flicks that became popular from mid-decade onwards. Typical offerings were **Invasion of the Saucermen** (1957), in which small-town kids trap the aliens in their car headlights, and the deliriously awful **Teenagers From Outer Space** (1959), which rivals **Robot Monster** as the all-time rock-bottom film within the science fiction genre.

In **The Blob** (1958), which marked Steve

Below *Grant Williams grapples with a mousetrap to feed himself in Jack Arnold's brilliant sf adventure* **The Incredible Shrinking Man** *(1957).*

McQueen's starring debut, an alien proto-plasm lands in a small California town and begins to devour its inhabitants. McQueen and his hot-rodding friends meet blank disbelief when they tell the musclebrained authorities that a big Red Thing is on the prowl. Then the primeval ooze invades the local cinema, and alarm sets in.

Top *The Vampire (1957)*. **Center** *The Werewolf (1956)*. **Above** *Over-age Robert Vaughn took the title role in Roger Corman's imaginative variation on the post-holocaust theme,* **Teenage Caveman** *(1958). Vaughn described it as "one of the best worst films of all time".* **Right** *Steve McQueen surveys the handiwork of* **The Blob** *(1958).*

48

CHAPTER FOUR

Future Past

At the beginning of the 1960s it seemed as if science fiction cinema would resume the role it had filled in the 1930s, as a kind of supermarket for decorative elements employed to spice up films from other genres.

Nowhere was this more apparent than in the series of James Bond films, which began with **Dr. No** (1962). Bond's evil antagonist, played with icy relish by Joseph Wiseman, is a compelling mixture of Sax Rohmer's Fu Manchu (he is Oriental) and **Metropolis**' Rotwang (his hands, contaminated in nuclear experiments, have been amputated and replaced with metal claws). Like all the great serial villains, Dr. No's goal is world domination. The means – unavailable to Rotwang or the Lightning – is atomic blackmail. Thwarted by Bond, he boils to death eventually in the water churning around his atomic pile.

Science fiction gimmicks also crept into ostensibly political thrillers like John Frankenheimer's **The Manchurian Candidate** (1962), in which Chinese scientists plant a brainwashed dupe in the United States, programmed to assassinate the President-elect. The plan breaks down when the dupe grasps what is happening to him and rebels against it.

Frankenheimer pursued this theme in two more films. In **Seven Days in May** (1964), a member of the American military establishment resists his own "programming" and acts to prevent the armed overthrow of the US government. Both **The Manchurian Candidate** and **Seven Days in May** dealt with the public misuse of technology – brainwashing and media manipulation. **Seconds** (1966) focuses on its private misuse, when a middle-aged businessman discovers that the price of rejuvenation and a new life is exacted by imprisonment in the wrong body. A shadowy organization fakes his death and turns him into Rock Hudson. However, in time he realizes the futility of his new existence and begins to yearn for his former life. When the organization denies him the chance to reverse the process, he chooses to die rather than deny his real self. His body will be put to use in another of the company's fake accidents.

Grim echo

This grim vision found an echo 12 years later in Michael Crichton's **Coma** (1978), in which Geneviève Bujold discovers that a hospital is inducing patients into comas

Below *A laser sizzles towards Sean Connery in* **Goldfinger** *(1964).* **Right** **Dr. No**, *the extremely successful descendant of* **Metropolis'** *Rotwang.*

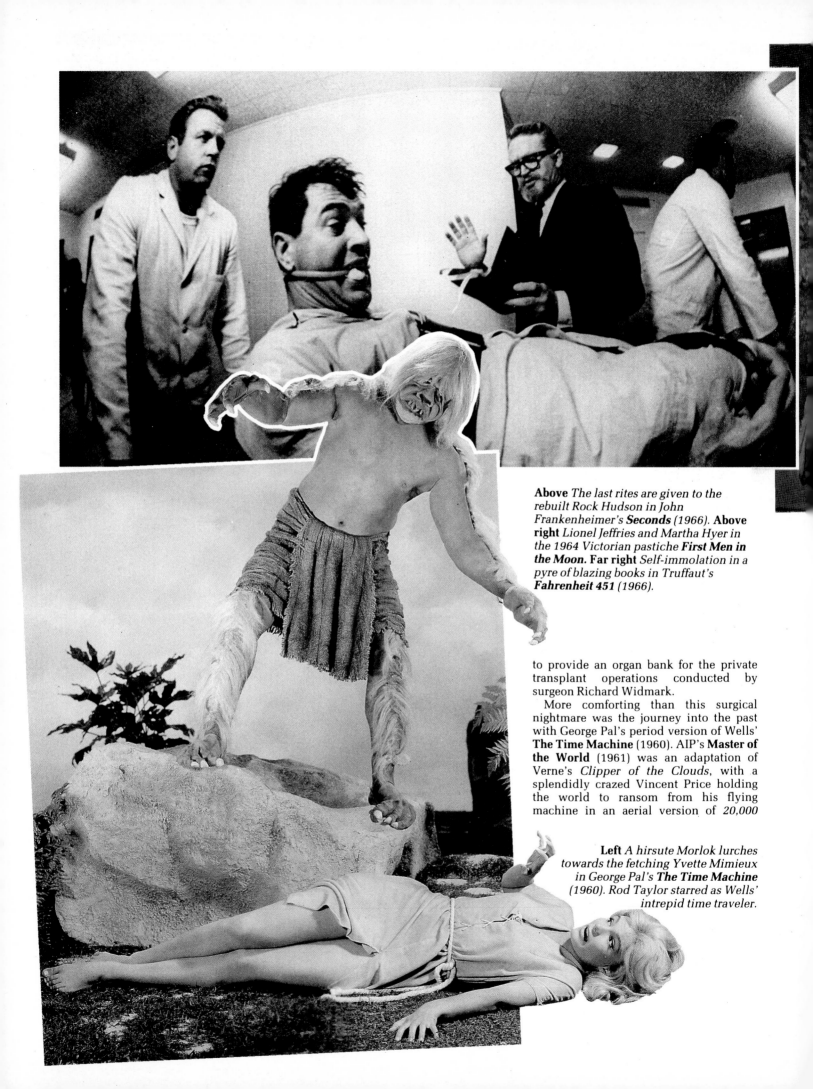

Above *The last rites are given to the rebuilt Rock Hudson in John Frankenheimer's* **Seconds** *(1966).* **Above right** *Lionel Jeffries and Martha Hyer in the 1964 Victorian pastiche* **First Men in the Moon.** **Far right** *Self-immolation in a pyre of blazing books in Truffaut's* **Fahrenheit 451** *(1966).*

to provide an organ bank for the private transplant operations conducted by surgeon Richard Widmark.

More comforting than this surgical nightmare was the journey into the past with George Pal's period version of Wells' **The Time Machine** (1960). AIP's **Master of the World** (1961) was an adaptation of Verne's *Clipper of the Clouds*, with a splendidly crazed Vincent Price holding the world to ransom from his flying machine in an aerial version of *20,000*

Left *A hirsute Morlok lurches towards the fetching Yvette Mimieux in George Pal's* **The Time Machine** *(1960). Rod Taylor starred as Wells' intrepid time traveler.*

Leagues Under the Sea. These were followed by Nathan Juran's cheerful **First Men in the Moon** (1964), based on the Wells novel that provided Méliès with the inspiration for **Le Voyage dans la Lune** and enhanced by Ray Harryhausen's excellent special effects.

Attempts to bring more recent science fiction classics to the screen were less successful. John Wyndham's *The Midwich Cuckoos* was given a pedestrian treatment by Wolf Rilla under the title **Village of the Damned** (1960). A variation on the "invisible invasion" theme, **Village of the Damned** was set in an English village whose inhabitants fall into a trance-like sleep for 24 hours. When they awake they find that all the women in the community are pregnant. The children they bear are aliens possessing fearsome telepathic powers. The film was virtually remade three years later as **Children of the Damned** (1963).

Sadly, in the same year, Wyndham's most famous novel, *The Day of the Triffids*, was completely mangled in its progress to the screen. The subtleties and specifically British flavor of the original – with its echoes of the Battle of Britain – were steamrollered into the ground by the substitution of a crass adventure story. The original screenplay was so bad that leading man Howard Keel rewrote most of his dialogue during filming. The Triffids, wobbling along looking like oversize clumps of broccoli, are a great disappointment.

Ray Bradbury's *Fahrenheit 451* fared little better in a fumbled 1966 screen treatment by François Truffaut. **Fahrenheit 451** is set in a future dystopia where all books are banned. Squads of firemen are employed to incinerate those that survive (the temperature at which paper will burn is 451 degrees Fahrenheit). Oskar Werner is the fireman who begins to have doubts about his job, seeks retreat in a secret hoard of books and finally joins "the book people", a community of fugitives who commit classics to memory in order to keep alive the spirit of free thought. This is Truffaut's weakest film, and his usual commitment to behavior seems at odds with the abstractions of science fiction. The credit for much of the film's visual quality, particularly the close-ups of burning books, must go to the cinematography of Nicolas Roeg.

Jean-Luc Godard was more at home with **Alphaville** (1965). Granite-faced Eddie

Constantine – a familiar B-feature hero – is the trench-coated intergalactic agent driving his late-model American car through "intersidereal space" to the alternative universe of Alphaville. The locations are the bleak suburbs of 1960s Paris and Constantine's Lemmy Caution is the hero of a thousand "hardboiled" private-eye novels. Lurking within this framework is a standard science fiction plot of a rogue computer, but the film's real purpose is to mesh together strands of classical mythology, comic strips and pulp fiction in a many-layered celebration of popular culture.

Back to the comic strip

Comic strip characters sprang vividly to life a couple of years later in two films: Mario Bava's **Diabolik** (1967) and Roger Vadim's **Barbarella** (1967). **Diabolik** is an immensely stylish science fiction thriller

in which John Philip Law was cast as the black-clad master criminal who at one point, bored with capitalism, destroys all of Italy's tax records. In a bravura finale he melts down a 20-ton radioactive gold ingot, only to have it explode, coating him in a shower of molten metal and transforming him into a living statue.

In **Diabolik** John Philip Law was limbering up for his role as the blind angel Pygar in **Barbarella**. Based on Jean-Claude Forest's risqué comic strip, this interplanetary erotic fantasy starred Jane Fonda as the innocent, Candide-like figure despatched to a wicked planet to rescue a missing scientist. The tone of the film is set in the opening sequence – a delicious freefall striptease – and clearly demonstrates Vadim's aim to turn Fonda, then his wife, into an international sex star.

Wide-eyed and delectable, Fonda retains her innocence as she moves through the voyeuristic fantasy world of Sogo, ruled by a vampire lesbian queen, where a new sin is invented every hour and contraptions like the Excessive Machine can literally pleasure its victims to death. *Flash Gordon* in drag, ravishingly photographed by Claude Renoir and extravagently designed by Mario Garbuglia, **Barbarella** remains an essentially humorous fantasy which contrives to resist its cynical center.

Left Jane Fonda with the blind angel Pygar in Barbarella (1967). **Below** *Barbarella with the planet Sogo's vampire queen (Anita Pallenberg).*

Aiming at the same target, but missing by a mile, was Mario Bava's **Dr. Goldfoot and the Girl Bombs** (1966), in which a would-be Dr. No played by Vincent Price at his most arch builds an army of sexy female robots programmed to assassinate NATO generals. The fuses are built into the robots' navels so that they will explode in the middle of the act of love. More serious in intent but equally silly was Richard Fleischer's **Fantastic Voyage**

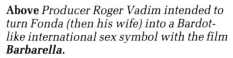

Above Producer Roger Vadim intended to turn Fonda (then his wife) into a Bardot-like international sex symbol with the film **Barbarella.**

(1966). In a medical version of **The Incredible Shrinking Man**, a submarine and its crew are miniaturized and injected into the bloodstream of an eminent scientist to deal with a clot of blood on his brain. Rather pompously, Fleischer declared that he wanted to "inspire young people with some understanding of the incredible complexity of the human body". Nevertheless, **Fantastic Voyage** stubbornly remains a psychedelic delight in the grand tradition of the 1960s.

The big breakthrough
At the end of the decade two films were released which, for better or worse, changed the momentum and course of science fiction cinema. The first was Franklin Schaffner's **Planet of the Apes** (1968), adapted by Rod Serling from Pierre Boulle's satirical novel *Monkey Planet*. A reworking of the time travel theme, it put Charlton Heston through a timeslip and on to a post-holocaust Earth in which intelligent apes have become the defenders of

"humanity". Firmly controlled by Schaffner, an old-fashioned craftsman, and strikingly photographed in Utah and Arizona, **Planet of the Apes** moves at a measured pace towards the memorable climax in which Heston finds the ruined, half-buried remains of the Statue of Liberty and comes to the bitter realization that he is on Earth after all.

Planet of the Apes was followed by the most influential science fiction film of the decade – Kubrick's **2001: A Space Odys-**

Left **Beneath the Planet of the Apes** *(1969), the sequel to* **Planet of the Apes** *(***below***), which was followed by* **Escape to the Planet of the Apes** *(1971),* **Conquest of the Planet of the Apes** *(1972) and* **Battle for the Planet of the Apes** *(1973).* **Below right** *the "ordinariness" of space travel in Kubrick's* **2001: A Space Odyssey** *(1968).*

sey (1968). Loosely adapted from his own story *The Sentinel*, by Arthur C. Clarke, it explored at greater length, and at far greater cost, the question taken up in **Planet of the Apes:** the forces which control man's evolution. A dazzling technical triumph, **2001** set out to restore speculative thought to science fiction cinema along with a sense of primitive wonder which harked back to the days of silent cinema. It succeeded so well that its images of vast, complex spacecraft floating with infinite slowness through deep space have now become clichés of modern cinema.

At its heart it contains one of the most stunning jump cuts in film – the moment when an animal bone hurled into the air by a prehistoric man is transformed into a slowly turning spaceship. It is perhaps in this technical mastery – from the intricately choreographed spaceship sequences to

the hallucinogenic passage through the star gate which precedes Keir Dullea's rebirth as a "transcended" man – that **2001**'s greatest achievement lies. Just as with David Lean's enormously expensive and painstakingly constructed blockbusters, **2001** does not stand up to close scrutiny as a film of ideas. It is something less than the sum of its calculatedly ambiguous pretensions, with the majestically manipulated hardware cloaking the shrivelled imagination at its center. Finally, it remains a deeply pessimistic film, an impression heightened by Kubrick's clinical distancing effect which reduces the human figures to mere ciphers.

Man may be ingenious – as instanced in the sequence when Keir Dullea dismantles the rogue computer HAL – but ultimately he is the passive object of the relentless force represented by the film's mysterious monolith.

CHAPTER FIVE

Galactic Megastars

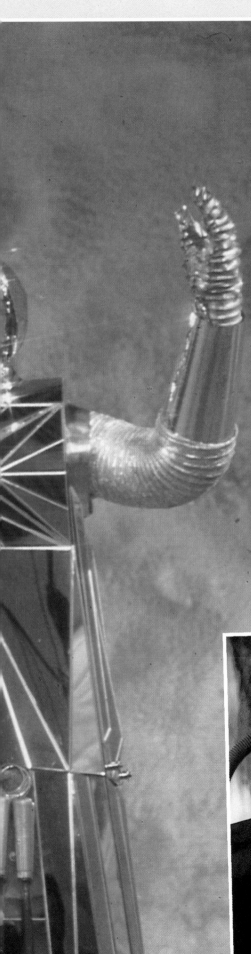

The phenomenal success of **2001** and **Planet of the Apes** swept the science fiction film into the 1970s on the crest of a wave. Once again producers were drawn towards the genre, a process that was hastened by the spiraling cost of Hollywood films and the decreasing number being made each year. Science fiction now fulfilled one invaluable criterion for producers. They could see at a glance where the money was being spent: on special effects. In the past it had been precisely the high cost of special effects that had worked against science fiction films. Now, when swollen budgets became the norm in mainstream filmmaking, the old drawback became a persuasive point in science fiction's favor.

This seismic shift in the financing of films can be seen at work in Robert Wise's **The Andromeda Strain** (1971), in which a US government scientific team sets out to locate and destroy an alien microorganism which has arrived on Earth on board a crashed satellite. Wise spent most of his $6.5 million budget on the vast underground isolation center hollowed out beneath the New Mexico desert to deal with the crisis. Despite the outlay, the most eerily effective moments in the film are the atmospheric exteriors shot in a ghost town.

Costly disasters

As every film producer knows, a big budget cannot guarantee success, and the 1970s saw a number of expensive, thudding science fiction failures. The plodding **Soylent Green** (1973), memorable only for the last appearance of Edward G. Robinson, and the mind-numbing **Logan's Run** (1976) demonstrated that production values are no substitute for imagination. Norman Jewison's **Rollerball** (1975) is big-budget science fiction at its most inept. **Rollerball** is set in the nearish future, 2018, when the world is controlled by a group of multinationals who keep the masses lobotomized with the time-honored Roman technique of "bread and circuses".

The circus in the film is a fiendish combination of football, hockey, roller derby and gladiatorial combat. James Caan is the rugged free spirit whose success on the Rollerball circuit threatens the system, which demands that its popular heroes

Inset and left *Logan's Run (1976), directed by Michael Anderson. Michael York and Jenny Agutter on their way to discovering that life begins at 30.* **Below** *The Andromeda Strain (1971), directed by Robert Wise.*

*Above Richard Fleischer's **Soylent Green** (1973) set in an overpopulated New York whose inhabitants survive on synthetic food manufactured from human corpses.*

rise and fall with metronome regularity. The brutish Caan climbs over a wall of corpses to beat the equally brutish system. Trapped in the coils of its own clumsy logic, **Rollerball** ends up celebrating the surrogate violence it sets out to condemn.

Rollerball, **Soylent Green** and **Logan's Run** present us with various forms of dystopia – the opposite of a Utopia. In **Soylent Green** the teeming hordes of an overpopulated world are fed with the synthetic foods manufactured by another sinister corporation. **Logan's Run** is a tale of youthful rebels set in an antiseptic Disneyland world of the future where everyone over 30 is neatly disposed of in a so-called "renewal ceremony". (This itself is an echo of such youth cult films of the 1960s as **Wild in the Streets**, in which those under 30 seize the reins of power.) Michael York is the "runner" whose task it is to stop those fleeing from "renewal" from reaching the mythical "sanctuary" outside.

A dystopia far closer to home is the tawdry police state in Kubrick's **A Clockwork Orange** (1971), adapted by Anthony Burgess from his own novel. Malcolm McDowell is the psychopathic gang leader forced to go through an appalling aversion therapy course "to save him from himself". No sooner is he released by the authorities, cowed and impotent, than they decide to restore him to his former self for the sake of temporary political convenience. Similar ground is covered by the more modest **The Terminal Man** (1974), directed by Mike Hodges. George Segal is the psychotic who has a tiny

behavior-controlling computer implanted in his brain.

The operation backfires as Segal finds the process of being "calmed down" so pleasurable that he embarks on a murdering spree to repeat the experience of being restrained. Man and machine are linked in a self-destructive spiral. McDowell's violence, however disgusting, is presented as the mark of a free will in a totalitarian society. Well-meaning doctors operate on Segal, but he remains just the same. McDowell in the end survives while Segal is hunted down and killed.

*Below **Rollerball** (1975) provided the spectator sport of the future in which the battle-scarred star player defeats the odds stacked against him by the system.*

Low-rent space travel

The immensely costly pretensions of **2001** inevitably produced a critical response from some film makers. In the intriguing German feature **The Big Mess** (1970), the Suez Canal Company – the ultimate multinational – controls all the economic activity in the Milky Way. A small band of adventurers is permitted to ply the more hazardous routes in its worn-out spacecraft. But free enterprise remains an illusion, as in reality everything is controlled by the Company, whose lust for materials and money is insatiable. The result is a plausible view of the future, combining high technology with the greed and stupidity which are the bottom line of human behavior.

The ramshackle, degrading hardware of **The Big Mess** is the central motif of John

Carpenter's feature film début **Dark Star** (1974). Shot over a period of three years on a budget of $60,000, the film is set aboard a junk-strewn spacecraft whose mission is to destroy unstable stars with its "talking" bombs. The captain is frozen in suspended animation – when woken up for advice in a crisis he tetchily demands the latest baseball scores – and the computer is on the blink. The ship is finally blown to oblivion by one of the "talking" bombs whose growing interest in philosophy leads it to the final, irrefutable statement: "Let There Be Light!".

The interior of the space station in the Russian **Solaris** (1972) is equally seedy, although the film's intellectual ambitions rival those of **2001**. The planet Solaris is a giant brain that can communicate with the astronauts in orbit above, materializing in human form a trauma, dream or memory which still haunts them: a kind of cosmic

conscience, perhaps, or an oblique metaphor for God. Like **2001**, **Solaris** falls into the trap of cloaking its romantic clichés in a visual and directorial *tour de force*.

Fifties nostalgia

Linked with the sardonic ripostes to Kubrick's grand designs are the low-budget quickies that look back to the freewheeling days of the 1950s. No one was faster off the mark than Roger Corman, whose engagingly tacky schlock epic **War of the Satellites** (1957) was rushed out to cash in on the launching of the first Soviet Sputnik. Nearly 20 years later Corman and his New World Company had lost none of their ability to beat the heavyweights to the punch. **Rollerball** bit the dust, but New World's cheerful rip-off **Death Race 2000** (1975) – in which a collection of maniacal drivers compete in the Transcontinental Death Race – cleaned up at the box office.

In the feature début of Australian director Peter Weir, **The Cars That Ate Paris** (1974), there was an equally tongue-in-

cheek view of an auto-dominated society. Cruising through the streets of a remote outback town are menacing columns of cars, weirdly encrusted with the cannibalized remains of vehicles lured to their destruction by the locals. For good measure the town doctor is carrying out a series of none-too-successful experiments on the hapless drivers who survive the crashes.

In part, **The Cars That Ate Paris** is a sly dig at anodyne Disney films like **The Love Bug** (1961) which featured a winsome little VW. In like fashion, Jeff Lieberman took a well-aimed sideswipe at the 1960s "flower generation" in **Blue Sunshine** (1977). A decade after *Sergeant Pepper*, their middle-class lives disintegrate as the long-delayed side-effects of a particularly virulent form of LSD transform them into bald, homicidal maniacs.

Nature, lying low since **The Birds** but still red in tooth and claw, also began to take its revenge, chiming with the increased interest in ecology. In **Frogs** (1972), a small army of swamp creatures

Right *Malcolm McDowell and his fellow droogs in Stanley Kubrick's* **A Clockwork Orange** *(1971), a characteristically bravura exercise in cynical style.*

puts a damper on Southern patriarch Ray Milland's birthday celebrations. **The Night of the Lepus** (1972) provided some of the more pervesely appealing monsters of the decade – giant, man-eating rabbits, swollen to the size of mules by a new pest control serum. In the grand tradition of the 1950s "creature feature", they are destroyed on a hastily electrified section of railway track. In **Phase IV** (1973), ants beseige mad scientist Nigel Davenport and his companions in his laboratory. The equally crazy scientist of **Bug** (1975) – a manic performance by Bradford Dillman – crosses a cockroach with a mysterious fire-producing insect thrown up in an earthquake and finds big trouble on his hands. New World's **Piranha** (1978) was a gleeful homage to **Jaws** in which a shoal of killer fish, reared at a US military establishment for use in Vietnam, eat their way through the patrons of a water sports facility.

Squirm ... and squirm again

Jeff Lieberman's **Squirm** (1976) features a host of carnivorous worms that surround an isolated farmhouse after a fallen power cable gives them a taste for flesh. **Squirm** is full of the quickfire black jokes that adorn all the best science fiction and horror exploitation films: at one point a sheriff wolfs down a plate of spaghetti while listening disbelievingly to the tale of the worms that have turned. Even more unsavory is David Cronenberg's **Shivers** (1974), in which a parasite infection transforms the residents of a middle-class housing complex into raving maniacs. Both phallic and scatological, the parasites represent an overwhelming disgust with sexuality – the mirror image of **Barbarella**'s coyly prurient eroticism or the camp antics of **Flesh Gordon** (1974), a sexploitation remake of Universal's classic 1936 serial.

The fate of the successful exploitation film is first to become a cult and then to enter the mainstream with a more lavish sequel. This was the route taken by George Miller's **Mad Max** (1979), a pared-down post-holocaust action flick set in the Australia of the near future. Violence is the norm, dwindling reserves of gas are the only units of exchange and the outback has become a battleground littered with the gutted hulks of the vehicles of biker gangs and the brutal representatives of what remains of the law. The Mad Max of the title is Mel Gibson, a policeman who finally goes berserk when his family is butchered. Miller makes only a perfunctory attempt to fill in the background to the film. All the energy is poured into the fast-paced action sequences.

An assured exercise in pure style, **Mad Max** was followed by a splendid sequel, **The Road Warrior** (1981). A kind of holocaust Western, it finds Gibson riding to the rescue of the last representatives of civilization, who are besieged in a desert fortress by an army of freaks under the command of a giant, the Humungus, who strides around in a steel mask and studded jockstrap. Directed at frantic pace and filled with relentlessly stylized violence which just manages to stay on the right side of parody, **Mad Max 2** is one of the most influential genre movies of the last five years, inspiring such imitations as **Battle Truck** (1982), **Turkey Shoot** (1982) and **Stryker** (1983).

Man and his machines

The notion of machinery that dwarfs the humans who operate it is as old as **Metropolis**. The machine of our age is the computer. When it is as intelligent as HAL in **2001**, it is quite capable of reaching the conclusion that it is innately superior to its unreliable creators. HAL is one of the greatest villains of science fiction, and his

Above *The pool runs red in* **Piranha** *(1978), which bared a jaunty fang or two in the direction of* **Jaws**. **Below and right** *David Cronenberg's* **Shivers** *(1974), in which a parasite plague turns the inhabitants of a condominium into blood-spattered maniacs.*

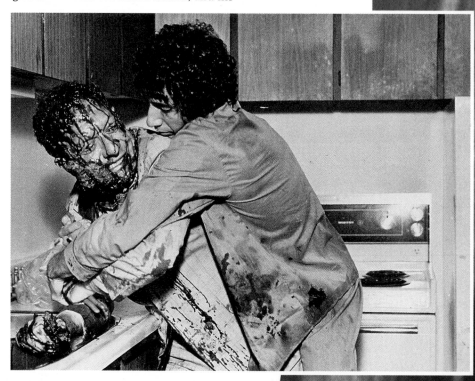

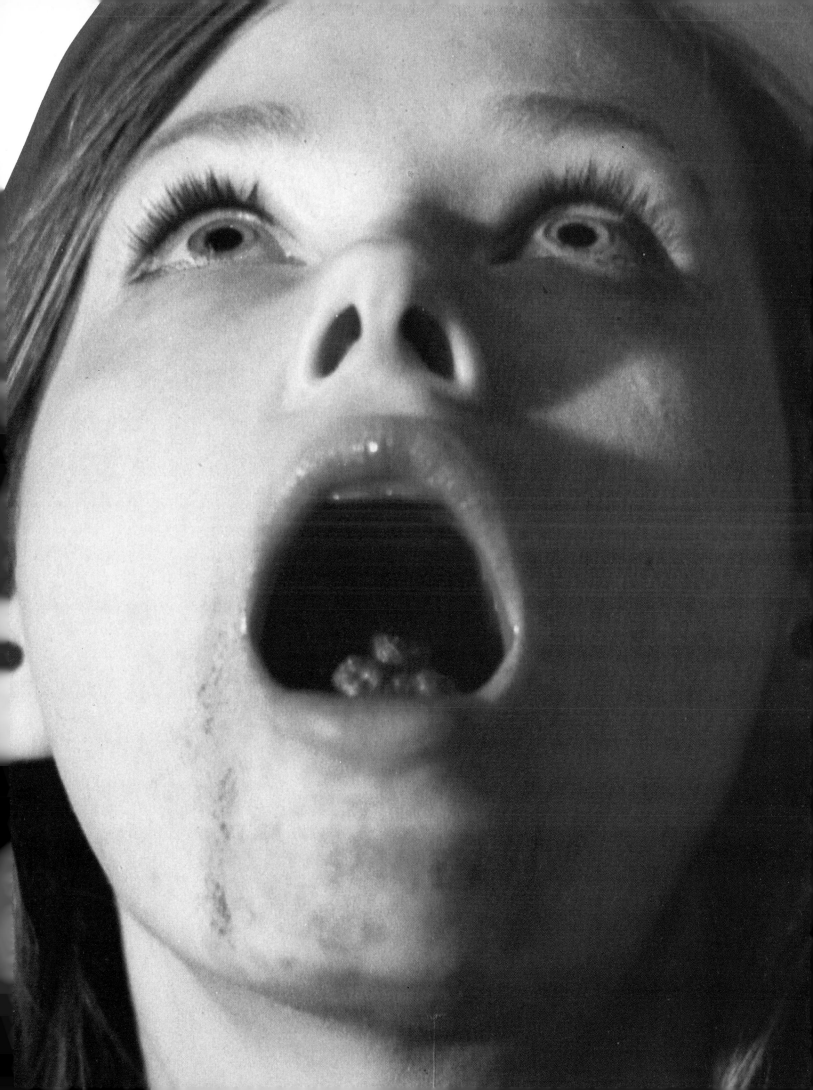

Below and right *Mad Max 2 (1981)*, directed by George Miller and one of the infrequent examples of a sequel improving on the original. Its gleefully exotic parade of fetishism and near-parodic super-violence have spawned a host of imitators.

anguished descent into simple-mindedness as he is disconnected by Keir Dullea has a genuine tragic quality. As he pipes the song taught him by his programmer, "Daisy, Daisy, Give Me Your Answer Do", he seems more human than his blank-faced adversary. In **2010** (1985), after an inordinate build-up, he is reconnected and, rather disappointingly, turns out to be a reformed character.

In **The Forbin Project** (1969), a giant US defense computer links up with its Russian counterpart in a bid for world domination. In the melodramatic **Demon Seed** (1977), the super-computer Phase IV manages to father a robot baby on an understandably distressed Julie Christie. Humans are not always on the receiving end of such unwonted attentions. In David Cronenberg's **Scanners** (1980), the paranormal Stephen Lack uses a telephone to probe the nervous system of a computer, with explosive results. Jeff Bridges went one further in Disney's **Tron** (1982), boldly going down the mean streets of a computer's circuits to joust with its power-crazed Master Control Program.

It is an axiom of the science fiction film that man's creations have a fatal tendency to run amok or turn against him. In Michael Crichton's **Westworld** (1973), the

*Left and above **2010** (1985), directed by Peter Hyams. A joint Russian/American expedition voyages to Venus to probe further the mysteries of the black monolith. At the film's climax HAL the computer makes the supreme sacrifice.*

robots that provide the holidaymakers in a futuristic Disneyworld with their ration of surrogate sex and violence suddenly go haywire. Bland businessman Richard Benjamin discovers that the Wild West gunslinger (Yul Brynner) is really out to shoot him down. The film's principal asset is Brynner as the grim-faced robot, a role for which he was cast by Nature. In an equally shrewd move the producers of **The Terminator** (1985) cast the musclebound bodybuilder Arnold Schwarzenegger as an indestructible android hit-man.

Robots can display a gruesome capacity for violence. Hector, the eight-foot superrobot of **Saturn 3** (1980), takes an equal delight in tearing living things apart and probing the more fascinating regions of Farrah Fawcett's body. In **The Return of the Jedi** (1983), a torture chamber's skeletal robot guardian dismembers the shrieking metal of lesser models in a compelling vision of replicant sadism.

Top and above *Wired: Julie Christie in the grip of the rogue computer, Phase IV, in* **Demon Seed** *(1977).* **Right** *Programmed to destruct — David Cronenberg's* **Scanners** *(1980), in which the humans of the title have the dreadful power to lock into another's central nervous system with explosive results.*

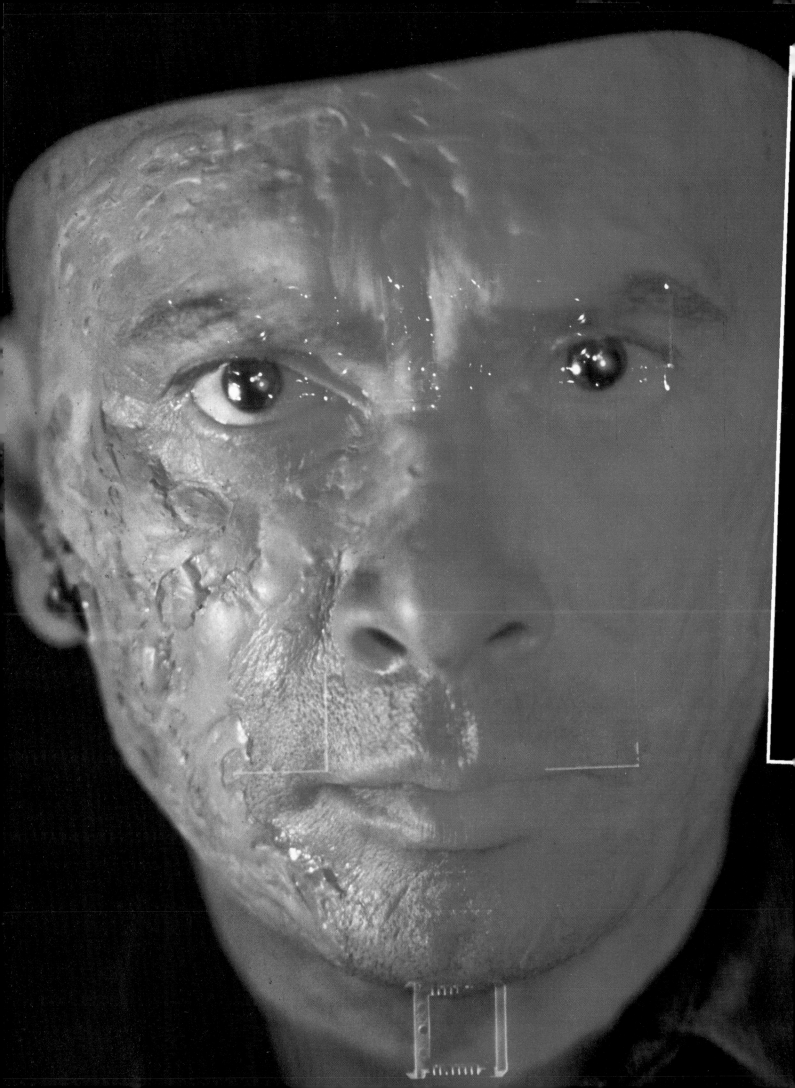

Far left *Melt down: Yul Brynner as the robot gunslinger in Michael Crichton's* **Westworld** *(1973).* **Above** *Dueling in* **Westworld** *with holidaymaker Richard Benjamin — soon it will be for real.* **Left** *In the sequel,* **Futureworld** *(1976), world leaders are replaced by robot lookalikes.*

Overleaf *Saturn 3 (1980), completed by Stanley Donen after the death of the original director John Barry and notable for the lustful interest its super-robot Hector displays in the helpless Farrah Fawcett. Special effects man Colin Chilvers modeled Hector on anatomical drawings by Leonardo da Vinci.*

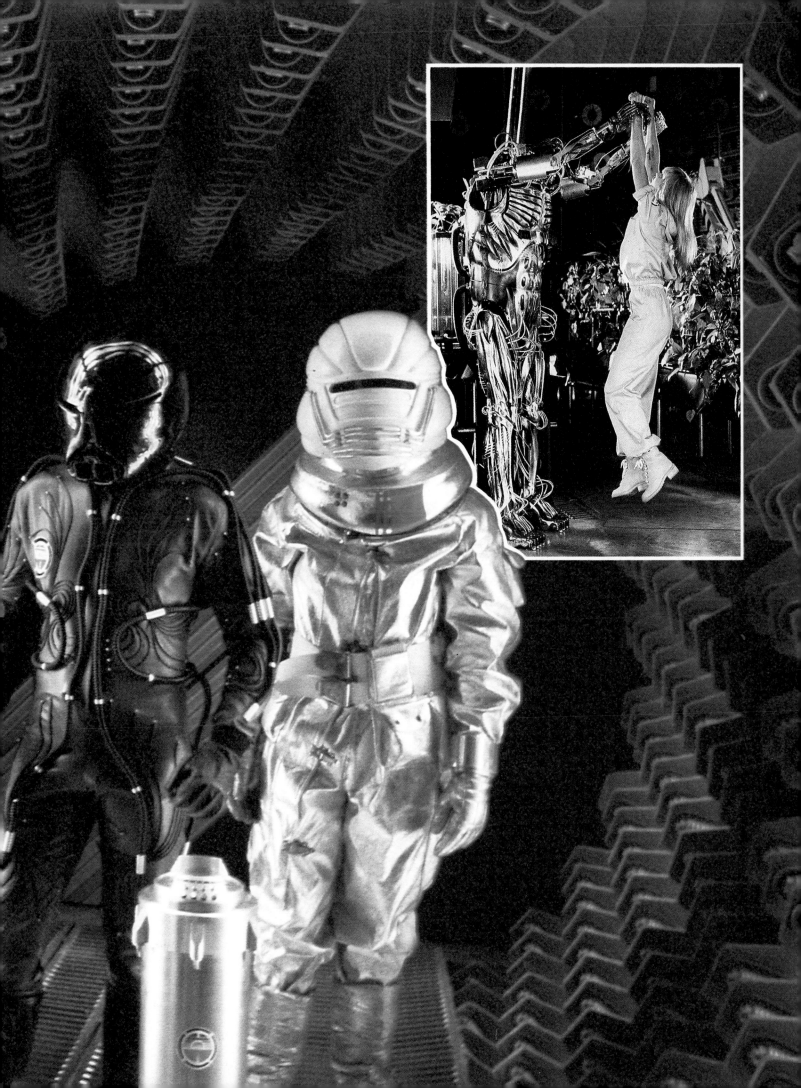

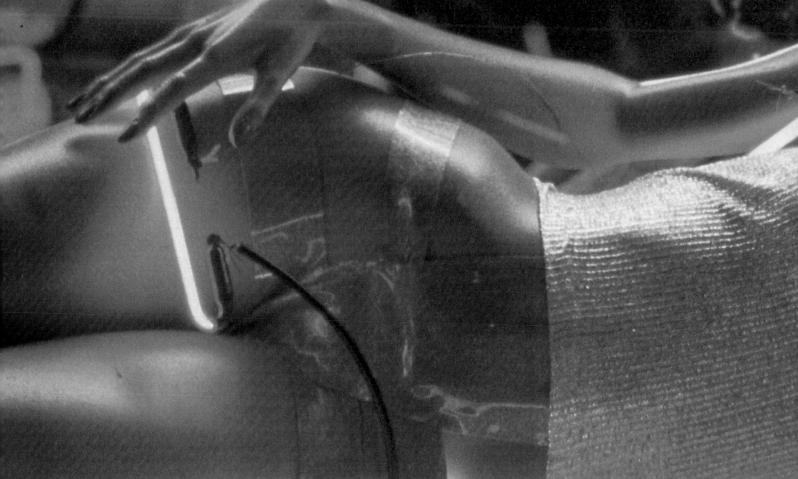

Butler with a difference

It is with relief that we turn to Woody Allen's **Sleeper** (1973), in which at one stage he is featured as an endearingly inefficient robot butler. The theme of robotic domesticity was pursued in Alan Arkush's charming, whimsical **Heartbeeps** (1981). Andy Kaufman and Bernadette Peters – heroically encased from head to foot in vacu-formed plastic – are two robot servants who begin to feel strange stirrings of emotion, build a spare-part robot "son" and complete their alternative family with "Uncle Catskill", a battered android comic who reels off an endless stream of Bortsch Belt wisecracks.

"Human" emotions also assail Max 404, the central character in Aaron Lipstadt's impressive directional début **Android** (1982). The floating space station which he shares with a Rotwang-like scientist (Klaus Kinski) becomes the refuge for a trio of escaped criminals. He falls in love with one of them, and in one of the film's most delightful conceits woos her in the style of James Stewart in Frank Capra's **It's a Wonderful Life** (1946), a movie to which Max has devoted many hours in his innocently earnest researches into life on Earth. At the conclusion of their first sexual encounter, his human partner tells him, "Max, you're a doll!". After a succession of adventures, including a grim interlude in which Max is temporarily reprogrammed to become a cold killer, he sets off to Earth with a new android girlfriend, hoping to carve out a life as a human. Oh, brave new world!

Equally poignant is the moment in **Spacehunter: Adventures in the Forbidden Zone** (1983) when interstellar adventurer Peter Strauss dicovers that his dying lover is a robot.

An android might be programmed with sufficiently sophisticated human responses to convince him that he is, indeed, human. This possibility hovers in the shadows of Ridley Scott's **Blade Runner** (1982). Harrison Ford is the hard-boiled bounty hunter on the track of a band of semi-human robot replicants through the trash-piled, steam-shrouded streets of a decaying twenty-first-century Chinatown.

The replicants' lifespan is limited to four years, precisely so that they will not get ideas above their station. They are direct descendants of Homunculus, a combination of instinctive animal grace and balletically explosive violence directed vengefully against their human creators. Fighting to stay the hand of the executioner, these exquisite creatures engage our

Left and below *Blade Runner (1982), loosely derived from Philip K. Dick's novel* Do Androids Dream of Electric Sheep? *Directed by Ridley Scott, it combines the clichés of the private-eye thriller with the demands of big-budget science-fiction.* **Right** *Runaway (1985), directed by Michael Crichton, also takes up the theme of killer human replicants. It includes a novel gimmick – a heat-seeking bullet that pursues detective hero Tom Selleck round corners as relentlessly as an Exocet missile.*

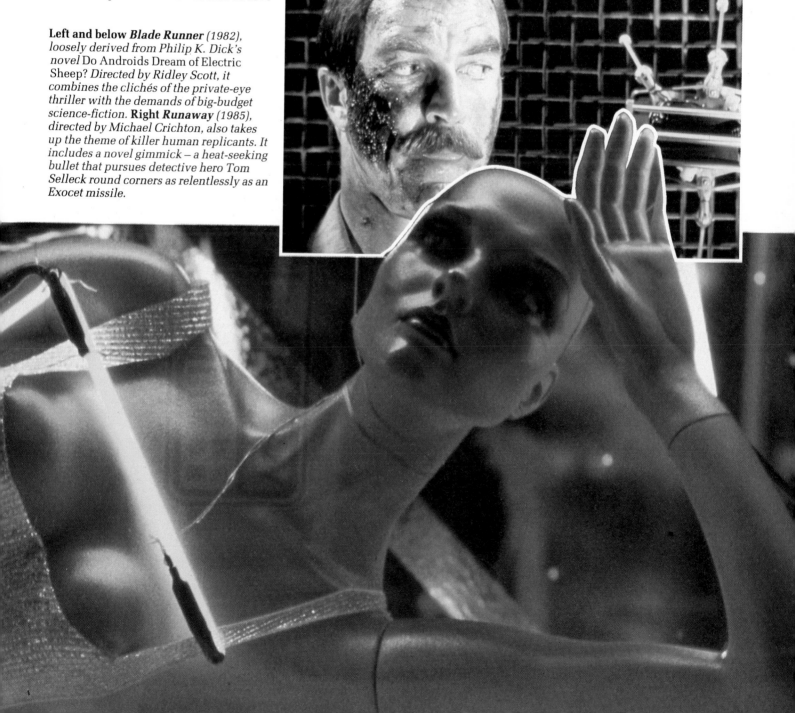

sympathy more readily than their pseudo-Bogartian pursuer who, ironically, might himself be a highly specialized android.

Star Wars and after

Just as **2001** had taken science fiction by the scruff of the neck in 1968, so **Star Wars** (1977) wrenched the genre into another quantum leap at the end of the 1970s. It also brought about a sharp change in the tone of the genre.

The more ambitious films of the decade had examined and questioned tendencies within our society. Now, pure fun, adventure and escapism were about to take over. As George Lucas has remarked of **Star Wars**, "the word for this movie is *fun* – I just wanted to forget science. That would take care of itself. Stanley Kubrick made the ultimate SF movie...I didn't want to make a **2001**...I wanted to make a space fantasy that was more in the genre of Edgar Rice Burroughs."

In common with Burroughs, the creator of Tarzan, Lucas is a consummate storyteller who is not afraid to borrow elements from a wide variety of sources to achieve his overall effect. The central threads of **Star Wars** are simplicity itself. Luke Skywalker leaves his uncle's farm on a small, arid planet on a quest to rescue a beautiful princess from the evil Grand Moff Tarkin.

Tarkin's henchman is Darth Vader. their base the Death Star, which is the size of a small moon and capable of destroying entire planets. Luke succeeds with the help of Obi-Wan Kenobi, a member of the mystical order of Jedi knights, a mercenary space pilot Han Solo and two endearing robots, R2-D2 and C-3PO.

Star Wars is an artful fusion of James Bond, the Western, SF serials of the 1930s, Errol Flynn swashbucklers and fantasies like **The Wizard of Oz**. The famous alien bar scene is lifted from a thousand horse operas, as is Luke's return to the homestead to find it burning and his family massacred. The climactic bombing runs down the narrow corridor to the heart of the Death Star recall the heroics of **The Dam Busters** (1955). **Star Wars**' bravura ending owed much to Leni Riefenstahl's **Triumph of the Will**.

But **Star Wars** is more than the sum of its eclectically gathered parts, and the broad outline framework laid down by Lucas – gutsy heroine Carrie Fisher, wise patriarch Alec Guinness, soft-hearted cynic Harrison Ford, earnest young hero Mark Hamill and his helpers, set against the evil Vader and the Death Star itself – has been refined into the status of myth in the two sequels.

The Empire Strikes Back (1980) pro-

vided Luke Skywalker with the knowledge that Vader was his father and Han Solo was left preserved alive, awaiting rescue, in a conclusion worthy of Flash Gordon. In the superbly mounted **Return of the Jedi** (1983), directed with great skill by Richard Marquand, Luke must fulfill his destiny by fighting his father to the death. At the last moment he stays his hand. Vader destroys the Emperor Palpatine at the cost of his own life. At the end of the **Return of the Jedi** Luke has attained tragi-heroic status. Like John Wayne's Ethan Edwards in **The Searchers** (1956), he has saved those around him but can find no peace for himself.

Space operas

Star Wars' brilliant computer-controlled camerawork, devised by John Dykstra, pushed back the boundaries of science fiction special effects. It also led to the development of Lucas' own vast special effects facility – Industrial Light and Magic, headed by Brian Johnson – a self-sufficient complex devoted to realizing the fantastic. The space operas that came close on **Star Wars**' heels found it a hard act to follow. It was also expensive.

The apex of special effects mismanagement was reached with **Star Trek – The Motion Picture** (1979) on which Para-

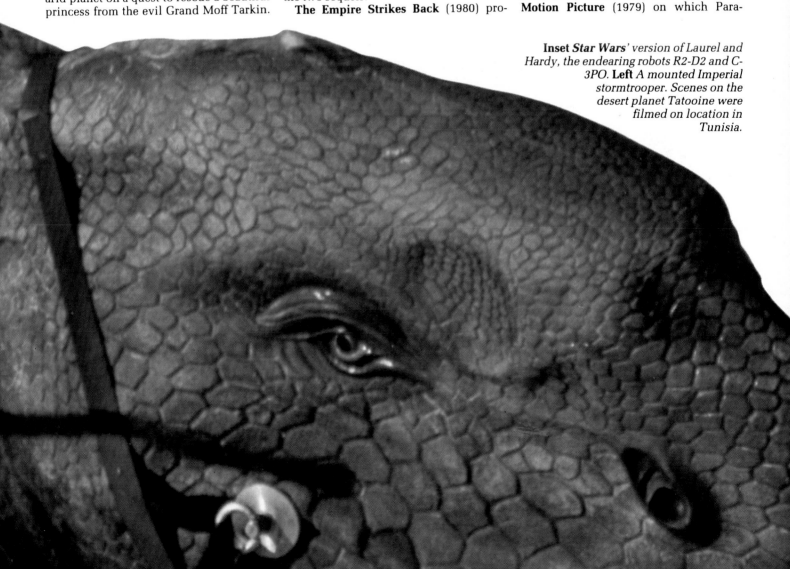

Inset *Star Wars' version of Laurel and Hardy, the endearing robots R2-D2 and C-3PO.* **Left** *A mounted Imperial stormtrooper. Scenes on the desert planet Tatooine were filmed on location in Tunisia.*

Above left *Luke Skywalker (Mark Hamill) confronts Darth Vader (David Prowse) in* **The Empire Strikes Back** *(1980), the second film in the* **Star Wars** *trilogy.* **Left** **Return of the Jedi** *(1983): Princess Leia (Carrie Fisher) in the clutches of the sand-dwelling omnivore Jabba the Hutt, whom she later strangles with a chain.* **Above** *Battle in space from* **Return of the Jedi** *(1983).* **Right** *The impish Jedi Master Yoda in* **Return of the Jedi** *(1983). Filled with no less than 945 separate special effects and brought to a superbly choreographed conclusion,* **Return of the Jedi** *propelled the* **Star Wars** *trilogy into the realm of myth.*

mount lavished $40 million to no discernible effect. The original budget had been slated for $5 million and the end result looked as if it had been made for less. For those operating at the frontiers of the art, the cost of the technology required to put a spaceship on the screen was spiraling towards the cost of the real thing.

Much of the domesticity of the teleseries was lost in the transfer to the big screen,

Left The Klingon commander in **Star Trek – the Motion Picture** *(1979).* **Above** *Still boldly going – the obsolete Enterprise in* **Star Trek III – the Search for Spock** *(1984), which was directed by Leonard Nimoy.* **Inset** *Ricardo Montalban, the villain of* **Star Trek II – the Wrath of Khan** *(1982). His captured spacecraft, the USS Reliant, makes an acronymic hint at Cold War divisions.*

although the thoughtful plot attempted to play on the series' principal strength in dealing with ideas rather than action. One of the more original touches was a bald alien leading lady (Persis Khambatta), a fetching corrective to the assorted toupees worn by the aging members of the Enterprise's flight deck.

Nevertheless, **Star Trek – The Motion Picture** emerged triumphant as a huge box-office hit. A sequel, **Star Trek II: The Wrath of Khan**, followed in 1982, with the Enterprise and her crew creaking back into action against the megalomaniac Khan, played by Ricardo Montalban like an Indian chief in a B Western. In thwarting Khan and his Genesis device Spock (Leonard Nimoy) makes the supreme sacrifice, only to turn up again in **Star Trek III – The Search for Spock** (1984), which Nimoy himself directed.

This time the obsolete Enterprise emerges illegally from mothballs and is pointed towards the final rendezvous on Vulcan with a reborn Spock. "Isn't your name...Jim?" he blearily asks Kirk after High Priestess Judith Anderson and a chorus line of diaphanously clad Vestal Vulcans have re-united him with his soul. The film ends with the caption, "And the adventure continues."

"Who's next?"

While **Star Trek**'s soothingly bland lines remained true to the 1960s original, Ridley Scott's **Alien** (1979) moved into the writhing, pulpy, phallic world of the surrealist artist H.R. Giger. Here the image is sexual rather than high-tech. Giger's version owes much to the tales of necromancy written at the turn of the century by H.P. Lovecraft, a pulp second-cousin to Edgar Allan Poe. It is in a planet full of these strange shapes that the crew of the Nostromo find the derelict spacecraft that contains the ultimately terrifying alien of

the title. Bearing a close resemblance to the 1958 cheapie, **It! The Terror from Beyond Space**, **Alien** remains – for all its sumptuous production values – a multi-million dollar second-feature variation on a number of tried and tested science fiction/horror B clichés. The film finally boils down to a simple question – "Who's next?"

"Who's next?" also became the overriding question in John Carpenter's remake of **The Thing** (1982) as the shape-shifting alien works his way through the members of the scientific team who have roused him from his 16-million year sleep in the arctic ice. **The Thing** moves from one special effects set piece to another, but without ever generating the tension of Hawks' original.

It must be said, however, that some of these gory *tours de force* are quite remarkable. In one scene electrodes are applied to a corpse in an attempt to start a heartbeat. In quick succession the body's torso sprouts fangs that bite off the arm of the terrified doctor; extends its neck like a concertina, lowering its head to the floor while at the same time sticking out an obscenely long tongue that wraps itself around a table leg. Finally it grows legs like a spider and scuttles away – to everyone's relief.

No-holds barred
The tyranny of special effects came under the characteristically mordant inspection of David Cronenberg in **Videodrome** (1982), which uses its frequently nauseating effects as a way of questioning the dubious morality of the no-holds barred pulp science fiction/horror films. Videodrome itself is a rogue television channel that literally warps the minds of those who watch it, inducing a form of cancer which brings in its train horrifying hallucinations. Its victims can no longer distinguish reality from fantasy. In one of the film's most disturbing images a sinister slit opens up in James Woods' belly ready to receive a cassette. He has become his own living video machine.

Alien (1979), directed by Ridley Scott, with the publicity line: "in space no one can hear you scream". **Left and below** *The Nostromo lands close to the huge alien spaceship, and the space-suited crew explore the derelict alien craft whose gaping orifices conjure up disturbing visions of a biomechanical world.* **Overleaf** *David Cronenberg's nightmarish* **Videodrome** *(1982), in which the dividing line between reality and fantasy disappears in a video dominated society.*

Dreams can come true

Star Wars aimed at recreating, and surpassing, the non-stop action of the classic serials of the 1930s. In **Close Encounters of the Third Kind** (1977) Steven Spielberg dug back farther and deeper, seeking to release in audiences the sense of wonder experienced by those who saw the miracle of moving pictures for the first time.

Close Encounters invokes the last words of Hawks' **The Thing** – "Watch the skies!" – but with none of the hysteria that runs through the science fiction film of the 1950s. The impulse behind the film is religious, a yearning to establish contact with the benevolent aliens rather than turn our guns on them in the manner of **Earth Versus the Flying Saucers**.

For the film's central character (Richard Dreyfuss) the journey to Devil's Rock in

Below *Cary Guffy bathed in the benign glow of the alien visitors in Steven Spielberg's* **Close Encounters of the Third Kind** *(1977).* **Right** *The arrival of the Mother ship at Devil's Tower, Wyoming.*

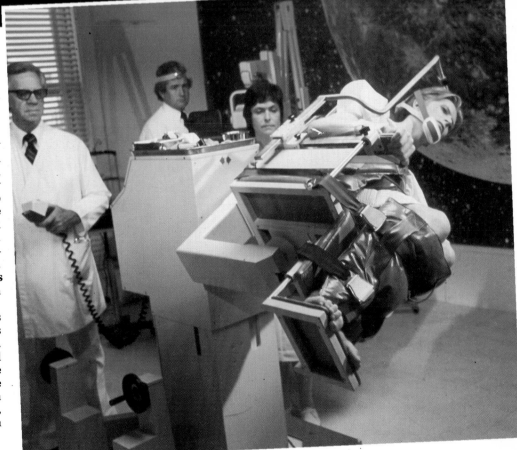

Right *David Bowie as the alien whose descent into humanity destroys him, strands him on Earth and dooms his own planet in* **The Man Who Fell to Earth** *(1976).*

Wyoming is a pilgrimage. Like a latter-day saint his own close encounter bathes him in the glow of the vision he has nourished along the way. Significantly, the military men who ring the landing site make no attempt to remove him when he joins the silent throng who watch with up-turned faces the descent of the Mother Ship. **Close Encounters** tells us that miracles – like the parting of the Red Sea in Cecil B. De Mille's **The Ten Commandments** (1956), glimpsed briefly on the television in Dreyfuss' living room – can come true.

   E.T. The Extraterrestrial (1982) has been accurately described by *Variety* as "the best Disney film Disney never made". Certainly it is Spielberg's most personal film and a powerful evocation of the innocent dreamworld of childhood, all the more seductive for being filtered through Spielberg's own instinctive grasp of myth, a quality that, ironically, he shares in abundance with Walt Disney.

E.T., the lost alien child who is befriended by the fatherless Elliott (E...T), becomes the invisible secret companion of all our childhoods. When the adult world intrudes it is viewed from a low angle – the child's point of view – a technique also used to great effect by William Cameron Menzies in **Invaders from Mars**. E.T. dies but, like Klaatu in **The Day the Earth Stood Still**, he reawakens in a plangent echo of the Resurrection of Christ. In a sequence that puts even the flintiest hearted to the test he teaches the children to soar above the clouds, freed from the rules and constraints of the adult world. It is an achievement of which Georges Méliès would have been suitably proud.

Far left *E.T. has phoned home – the space ship returns to collect the errant alien child mislaid on a previous visit to Earth in* **E.T. The Extraterrestrial** *(1982).* **Left** *E.T. finds a friend.* **Below** *Having escaped adult clutches, Elliott and his friend wait for the ship to land, when E.T. will rejoin his folks.*

*At the limits of the megabudget was David Lynch's ambitious attempt to film Frank Herbert's cult novel **Dune** (1984).*

Above *Emperor Shaddam IV welcomes the Spacing Guild Navigator.*
Inset *The evil Baron Harkonnen.*

Above *Krull* (1983), directed by Peter Yates, was a cheerful British blend of sword and sorcery and science fiction. **Left** *Space Valkyrie Sybil Danning in New World's* **Battle Beyond the Stars** (1980), which hijacked the plot of **The Magnificent Seven** (1960). **Below** *John Saxon in* **Battle Beyond the Stars**. **Right** **Brainstorm** (1983), directed by special effects wizard Douglas Trumbull. **Overleaf** *The ship Palamino heads straight towards* **The Black Hole** (1979).

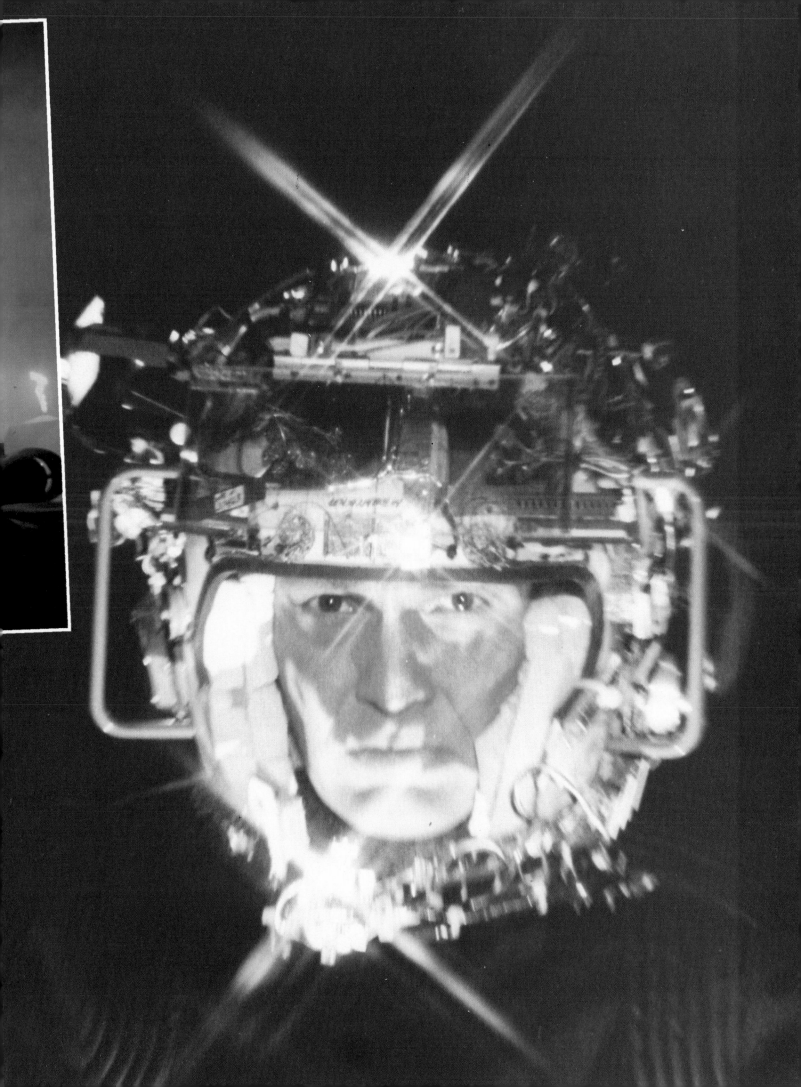

PICTURE CREDITS

Ronald Grant Archive 6-7, 8, 11 top, 17 top, 24, 26 bottom, 28 top, 33 top, 36 bottom, 42, 48 top, 48 middle, 50-51, 52 top, 53, 57, 58, 66, 67, 68 top, 71   **The Kobal Collection** half title, 7 bottom, 8, 9, 10-11, 12-15, 17-21, 23, 25, 26 top, 27, 28 bottom, 29-31, 34, 35, 38, 39, 40-41, 41 top, 42-43, 44-45, 46-47, 48-49, 52 bottom, 54, 55, 56-57, 59 bottom, 60 top, 62 bottom, 64-65, 68, 70, 73-75, 78 bottom, 79, 81 inset, 84-87, 88, 89, 90-91, 92 left, 92 right   **Alan McKenzie** title page, contents, 16, 22, 32, 33 bottom, 36 top, 40, 45 top, 45 bottom, 47, 48 bottom, 61, 62 top, 64, 68-69, 72-73, 76, 77, 78 top, 80-81, 81 top, 83, 92 top, 93, 94-95   **Ray Millard** 36-37   **National Film Archive** 28 middle   **Rex Features Limited** endpapers, 56 top, 60 bottom, 75, 90 top

Front and Back Cover: **Alan McKenzie**

ACKNOWLEDGEMENTS

Many of the illustrations come from stills issued to publicize films or distributed by the following companies:– Allied Artists/Wanger, American International, Columbia/EMI, EMI, Hammer Pictures, ITC, Joel Productions Inc. Presentation, Paramount Pictures, Twentieth Century Fox, UFA, United Artists, Universal City Studios Inc, Universal Pictures, Warner Brothers

Multimedia Publications (UK) Limited have endeavored to observe the legal requirements with regard to the rights of suppliers of photographic material.